9.07

D1270776

W. Robertson Smith
and the Sociological Study
of Religion

T. O. Beidelman

With a Foreword by
E. E. Evans-Pritchard

The University of Chicago Press

Chicago and London

T. O. BEIDELMAN is professor of
anthropology at New York University.
He has written *The Kaguru, The Matrilineal Peoples of Eastern Tanzania,*
and *A Comparative Analysis of the
Jajmani System.*

[1974]

The University of Chicago Press, Chicago 60637
The University of Chicago Press, Ltd., London

International Standard Book Number: 0-226-04158-1 (clothbound)
Library of Congress Catalog Card Number: 74-7568

To Lauren Brown,
with affection

Contents

Foreword

by E. E. Evans-Pritchard

Professor Beidelman has done me the honor, because he knows how much I admire W. Robertson Smith, of asking me to write a foreword to this book. I write a very brief one, for I do not see how the book can be improved upon, and when I had read it, I could only advise him not to alter a word of it. It is certainly the most exhaustive, and also discerning, assessment of Smith and his writings made in this century. I agree with Professor Beidelman that Smith's best contribution to Semitic scholarship was *The Prophets of Israel,* but that the books which made their greatest impact on social anthropology and Semitic studies were his *Kinship and Marriage in Early Arabia* and *Lectures on the Religion of the Semites.* Their influence spread far beyond social anthropology and Semitic scholarship, as witness Durkheim and Freud. Insofar as social anthropology is concerned, Smith is a key link in the chain (what the Arabs call *silsila*) of intellectual succession, ultimately from the moral philosophers of Scotland, mainly in Edinburgh, in the second half of the eighteenth century and the first decades of the nineteenth century. In particular, he was a vital link between McLennan, who in a strict sense was the first major writer in the history of social anthropology, and in that sense its founder, and Frazer, whose *Golden Bough* brought the subject into a wider circle of thought than that of specialist interest.

McLennan's influence was not always a happy one and sometimes blinded Smith to what could be inferred from the evidence. This is the case with what he wrote about what he supposed was matrilineal descent among the Bedouin of Arabia before the Prophet Muhammad, and likewise about what he regarded as their totemism; and his communion theory of the origin and meaning of sacrifice would, if accepted at all, be treated with reserve by most biblical scholars today. For some of these errors to be fully appreciated it is helpful to have a knowledge of at least Hebrew and Arabic. Since Professor Beidelman does not claim to have that knowledge, he has wisely avoided a discussion of linguistic matters, for these are deep waters in which anyone can drown; and much is still obscure and in dispute among Semitic scholars themselves. Even so great a scholar as Smith sometimes fell into traps. But if he sometimes misinterpreted the evidence, there is no question about his significance for the history of thought, especially for the history of social anthropological thought. Everyone can, and does, make mistakes on certain points in a vast amount of writing. If not, how could we have made any advance in our researches since? It is the old story of pygmies on the backs of giants seeing further than the giants themselves.

Preface

William Robertson Smith's interest in the sociological study of religion can only be fully appreciated if we understand his personality and career. Although an extensive biography was published in 1912, this has long been out of print and is not readily available to many students and scholars. In any case this earlier biography is essentially a narrative, eulogistic account with little attempt to relate Smith's character and background to his work and influence. Furthermore, some useful biographical information has been subsequently published. It seems proper, therefore, to begin this study with a biographical sketch which emphasizes those aspects of his life and background which appear to have been most influential in forming his character and intellectual outlook.

In any attempt to understand the significance of Smith's work in the sociology of religion, it is also essential to relate it to that of his contemporaries, including his friend John McLennan and his protégé Sir James Frazer, and to Smith's enormous yet generally unappreciated impact upon French sociology, mainly through Durkheim and Mauss. In reviewing both the intellectual influences upon Smith and his impact upon those who followed him, one must take some account of both biblical and Semitic scholarship, as well as work in social anthropology; unfortunately, I can make no claims to any competence in the highly technical and complex fields of biblical and Semitic studies. However, I have tried to indicate what influences Smith himself saw as important, and I have cited a few useful critical sources that survey and evaluate some of the basic issues with which Smith was concerned.

Few if any would claim that Smith, despite his fantastic erudition and controversial celebrity, was a genuine innovator in the fields of biblical or Semitic literary studies; rather, he introduced and popularized in Britain revolutionary interpretations in these fields already formulated by Continental scholars, especially in Germany and Holland. It is in the field of the sociology or psychology of religion that Smith's work is significant. In this sense, at least, the broader value of his theories and views may be considered apart from the detailed accuracy of his information on Semitic texts. It is in his views on the interrelationship between human psychology, social structure, and history that his most enduring contributions lie.

With this in mind, I have tried, finally, to indicate the ways in which Smith may still be read with profit, both because (for better or worse) some of his theories persist in much contemporary social analysis of religion and also because his arguments and expositions, enhanced by his lucid and forceful prose, often provide excellent models for emulation, in their fine scholarship, in their often highly original and imaginative insights, and perhaps most of all, in Smith's refreshingly interdisciplinary approach, in which he saw no parochial restrictions separating good social science, good history, good linguistics, and good theology. Indeed, for Smith theological study was a science, and his dislike of contemporary theologians was related to their failure to become scholars in the disciplines which affected their problems. For Smith, knowledge and criticism could only provide a surer and purer form of religious truth.

The text of the *Lectures on the Religion of the Semites* cited in this study is that of the second edition (1894) rather than the first (1889), since this is the final version which Smith prepared, greatly expanded from the first and presumably improved in form and content. This is the version which has appeared in all subsequent editions and printings and the one utilized by nearly all of the authorities cited in the discussion.

I should like to thank Ms. Helen Anderson of the *Encyclopaedia Britannica* for providing information on the ninth edition; Mr. M. J. D. Newth of Adam and Charles Black, Publishers, for very useful information about the history of that firm and for his general help and suggestions regarding this publication; Mrs. S. Victory, secretary to the librarian of Christ's College, Cambridge, for information on Smith's career at Cambridge; the librarians of the National Library of Scotland, Edinburgh, and of the University Library, Edinburgh University, for their advice and help; Ms. B. J. Kirkpatrick, librarian of the Royal Anthropological Institute, for a reference to Sir Richard Burton; Mr. Frank Cooper for help in collating texts of different editions of the

Lectures; Dr. Dale Eickelman, Professor John Middleton, and Dr. Rodney Needham who have all been kind enough to read various drafts of the manuscript. I am particularly grateful to Dr. Needham for having first suggested that I undertake this study.

Abbreviations

Throughout the text and the Bibliography the following abbreviations have been used:

BFE	*British and Foreign Evangelical Review.* Edinburgh.
EB	*Encyclopaedia Britannica.* 9th ed. Edinburgh and London: A. and C. Black, 1875-88.
EBL	*Encyclopaedia Biblica.* London and New York: Macmillan, 1899-1903.
LE	*Lectures and Essays of William Robertson Smith.* Edited by John Sutherland Black and George Chrystal. London: A. and C. Black, 1912.
Life	J. S. Black and G. W. Chrystal. *The Life of William Robertson Smith.* London: A. and C. Black, 1912.
LRS	W. Robertson Smith. *Lectures on the Religion of the Semites.* 2d ed. London: A. and C. Black, 1894.

W. Robertson Smith
and the Sociological Study
of Religion

A little controversy does one good. — *W. Robertson Smith*

He that believeth shall not make haste. — *Isaiah 28: 16*

W. Robertson Smith
and the Sociological Study
of Religion

BIOGRAPHICAL SKETCH

The Early Years

William Robertson Smith was born on Sunday, 8 November 1846, at New Farm in the parish of Keig, Aberdeenshire, Scotland. Only a year before, his father, William Pierie Smith, had, after an earlier career as headmaster of a school, been ordained a minister in the Free Church of Scotland, a more conservative offshoot of the National Church of Scotland, and had taken up residence in his first parish, Keig. William Robertson, the minister's first son, was named after his father and his maternal grandfather. He had an older sister, Mary Jane; three younger brothers, George, Charles, and Herbert; and two younger sisters, Nellie and Lucy. Although Smith's parents achieved old age, most of the children appear to have been somewhat frail and unhealthy, Mary Jane, George, and Herbert all dying of tuberculosis in their early youth. The disease was also to claim their famous brother at the age of forty-eight. Little is known of Nellie, Charles, and Lucy, who outlived William, except that Charles for a time served as government astronomer at Madras.

During a time when such qualities were assumed as proper to all in their class, contemporaries still remarked on the outstanding strength, tenacity, intellectualism, and sobriety of Smith's parents. Religious studies, the sciences, mathematics, and languages were fields for daily effort and discussion in the household, while the arts, even novels, appear to have been viewed more as indulgences than as fit subjects for prolonged attention.

The first of the two epigraphs on the facing page is a comment by Smith regarding a scholarly dispute between the Semitic scholars S. R. Driver and A. H. Sayce. It is quoted in J. S. Black and G. Chrystal, *The Life of William Robertson Smith* (London: A. and C. Black, 1912), p. 551. The second epigraph was inscribed by Smith on his favorite and best-known portrait, painted by his friend Sir George Reid.

William was soon recognized as remarkably bright, although with a high-strung temperament and fragile health. Lack of funds and the perpetual ill health of many of the children had led to their being tutored privately at home by their parents. The sparseness of population at Keig, moreover, forced the Smith children to rely upon themselves for their social life. By all accounts the children received a superb education, William learning to read some Hebrew when only five.

William entered Aberdeen University in 1861, when he was not quite fifteen, and was graded first in the entrance bursary examinations. His younger brother George also entered the university at the same time, and the two set up residence in Aberdeen town under the care of their eldest sister, Mary Jane. All three were tubercular, and given the meager food, long hours of study, harsh climate, and poorly heated lodgings and classrooms common at that time, the three must certainly have had a most difficult time. During the third year, Mary Jane died.

The brothers persisted in their studies, and, despite erratic class attendance during their final year due to ill health, both were considered outstanding scholars. William was too ill to take all of his final examinations, and George was examined in his sickroom, with a doctor in attendance. George died three weeks after graduation in 1865.

Despite these disasters, William received the Town Council Gold Medal as the most distinguished student of his year, and it was generally conceded by both faculty and student body that he would be a brilliant success in any field he was likely to choose. At Aberdeen he had shown extraordinary abilities in science, mathematics, and languages, especially the classic languages of theology. During his second year at college he had declared his intention of becoming a minister, in emulation of his father, but the next few years of his academic life continued to reflect his ambivalence regarding what his true interests and gifts in scholarship might be. George's tragic death remained in his thoughts, and it was considered by some to have in some way strengthened his intention to join the ministry.

In 1866, having received the Fergusson Scholarship in Mathematics and Classics, open for competition to all college students in Scotland, and the Fullerton and Moir Scholarship, open to students from Aberdeen, Smith enrolled at New College, Edinburgh, which had attached to it a seminary for the Free Church, to which his father belonged. He had waited for a year after graduating from Aberdeen before entering Edinburgh at the age of twenty; it had been felt by both his family and teachers that he was still somewhat young to embark on a theological career and that a year's pause would do both his mind and his health some good.

Preceded by a dazzling academic reputation, Smith took up residence at Edinburgh with his younger sister, Nellie, as housekeeper. At Edinburgh he managed to pursue both of his major interests, biblical studies and the natural sciences. He served as research assistant (along with Robert Louis Stevenson[1]) in the physics laboratory of P. G. Tait, professor of natural philosophy, and joined the Royal Society of Edinburgh, where he presented successful papers in physics and mathematics. Having worked during the summers with his father, he had greatly improved his Hebrew, which now flourished under the guidance of his favorite professor, A. B. Davidson, a distinguished Hebrew scholar at the seminary. Davidson advocated treating the biblical books as any other type of books, in that they should be subjected to the same techniques of textual criticism as would be applied to other ancient materials. This, of course, was the basic view of most sophisticated biblical scholars and was firmly adopted by Smith, but it was later to cause him serious difficulties with the more conservative members of the Free Church.

At Edinburgh Smith no longer drove himself with study in the same manner as before. At Aberdeen he had pursued nearly every subject with zeal. Now he tended to concentrate on those subjects that truly attracted him, especially mathematics and biblical studies. He is said to have cut classes, such as those taught by Principal Rainy, which he considered to be poorly conducted, preferring to master the material by intensive, independent reading. He became an active member in several Edinburgh discussion groups and clubs. His mentor, Professor Tait, relished lively discussion as much as Smith and introduced him to a

---

1. One may safely assume that Stevenson and Smith met. It is not at all clear what impression they had of one another, but later Stevenson referred to Smith in a negative manner: "Preacher on preacher, kirk on kirk—/This yin a stot an' thon a stirk—/A blet herin' clan, no warth a preen,/As bad as Smith o' Aiberdeen." These lines appear in Stevenson's poem "The Scotsman's Return from Abroad," first published in *Fraser's Magazine*, November 1880. I am indebted to Mr. E. J. Mehew for this reference. Stevenson's friend, W. E. Henley, a former employee of the *Encyclopaedia Britannica*, was known to dislike Smith and to have been indirectly responsible for some highly insulting essays attacking him. See *Life*, pp. 500-502.

wider circle of intellectuals, including John F. McLennan in 1869. It seems clear that the more challenging and sophisticated cultural life of Edinburgh encouraged Smith into a more sociable exercise of his gifts. He was a friendly person; what for some passed as unsociability was simply his refusal to expend his energies with those less seriously devoted to scholarship and service than he. Where he could find minds of his caliber, or even simply a person with a sincere desire to enquire and learn, there Smith remained a kind and genuine friend and teacher. One is struck by the enormous outlay of Smith's attention, throughout his career, in providing self-effacing assistance and advice to scholars, friends, and students.

In 1867, with the encouragement of A. B. Davidson, Smith wrote the first draft of his essay "Prophecy and Personality," the first public exposition of his views on biblical scholarship.[2] In this essay he wrote with striking originality and clarity upon a problem which continued to hold his attention throughout his career: the resolution of two aspects of prophecy, the absolute aspect by which prophets speak for God and thus express some external and unvarying truth, and the personal, idiosyncratic aspect grounded in their individual psychology and in the social milieu of their particular historical period. Smith returned to the theme in *The Prophets of Israel* (1882), perhaps the least dated and most attractive of his books.

In 1868, at the end of his first year at Edinburgh, Smith visited Bonn. It was the first of many visits he was to make to Germany and to other parts of the Continent. Smith easily mastered German as well as Dutch and French, and as he mixed with foreign scholars, his own views broadened, not only in theology but in biblical and Semitic studies, classics, mathematics, and physics. In biblical and Semitic studies, Germany led the world in what was then called "the new criticism." In 1869, Smith returned to Germany to study Arabic at Göttingen. During these visits to the Continent Smith learned to admire the German semiticists Lagarde and Wellhausen and the theologian Ritschl, as well as the Dutch biblical scholar Kuenen, and he began to take on a more eclectic, less dogmatic theological view.

2.   Although the essay was not properly published until after Smith's death, it was presented at a meeting of the Theological Society at Smith's college. I have not been able to determine whether a draft was circulated at that time or whether the society printed any such paper.

In autumn of 1869 Smith returned to Edinburgh to find that Professor Sachs, holder of the chair of Hebrew and Old Testament at the Free Church College at Aberdeen, had died. Davidson, Tait, and many of the younger staff members at Aberdeen, as well as Smith's friends on the Continent, pressed for his appointment. Smith took up the chair on 2 November 1870, being ordained in the Free Church ministry on the same day. In his inaugural lecture[3] he presented the ideas of the German school of new criticism, and during the following five years he argued for a freer, more historically accurate interpretation of the Bible. His lectures were well received among his students and, apparently, some of his colleagues, even though these same views were later to lead to his dismissal.

With his appointment, Smith continued to liberalize his style of life, making friends with an ever wider circle of scholars, artists, and scientists.

Smith's Character

Smith reached intellectual maturity at a very early age. Although his erudition increased with the decades, his views during his final years at Edinburgh and the first five years after graduation foreshadow many of the most basic notions which he developed in his later, more famous works. Consequently, a discussion of his years at Edinburgh flows smoothly into a discussion of his later distinguished career as an author and teacher. But before embarking on such a discussion it seems useful to provide some description of Smith's appearance, personality, and character, since these qualities are related to his intellectual achievements.

Smith's phenomenal academic attainments are undoubtedly the first of his qualities to strike any reader of his biography. In much the same way they dazzled his fellow students and teachers and, later, his own students and colleagues. In part these attainments were the result of an outstanding intelligence, amazing powers of memory, a highly orderly set of working habits, and a deep, driving sense of obligation to realize his full potentiality. This last was not out of any mere sense of self-advancement but out of a belief that this was both an obligation to

3.   Given November 1870, and published that year as *What History Teaches Us to Seek in the Bible* (Edinburgh: Edmonston and Douglas), 30 pages. It was reprinted in *LE*, pp. 207–34.

his parents, who held such high hopes for him,[4] and his obligation to God to develop fully whatever gifts he had been given, for to Smith knowledge and understanding were invariably equivalent to the praise and fulfillment of God's plans for men and for the possible achievement of a good life, that is, one pleasing to both men and God. What often seemed in Smith to be an almost overzealous distaste and impatience with pseudoscholarship and hack academics, an awesome overkill in scholarly controversies, suddenly becomes attractive and reasonable once one realizes that Smith truly saw slack scholarship and intellectual carelessness and laziness as profoundly immoral, an affront to man's potential and to God's gifts to us. And to Smith, the labor of scholarship, of sifting out evidence to learn the truth, was a way for men to gain the right and merit to reap the benefits of deeper knowledge of truth: "God who gave us the Bible has also given us faculties of reason and gifts of scholarship with which to study the Bible, and...the true meaning of Scripture is not to be measured by preconceived notions, but determined as the result of legitimate research."[5]

In his reviews and appraisals of serious scholars, Smith usually shows himself to be generous and judicious, even when he is in disagreement with them. But to opportunistic upstarts and panders to the generally uninformed, he was unremitting in his critical contempt: "When a half-informed person comes forward with pretensions and authority, when he claims to judge and condemn those who really know, and to do so from a standpoint of superior intelligence and information, it is not amiss to point out his mistakes, and if he has got the ear of the public it is sometimes a duty to do so."[6]

In his recollections of Smith, Reverend J. P. Lilley observes: "in all his earliest days Smith suffered from the lack of that discipline in patience and forebearance which is best attached through the intercourse of a large public school. Hence he was often prone to pass sharp

4. Smith appears to have been very closely attached to both of his parents, and their painted portraits dominated his study at college.

5. *The Old Testament in the Jewish Church* (New York: Appleton, 1881), pp. 27-28. See also "The Progress of Old Testament Studies," *BFE* 25 (July 1876): 471-93. This paper represents a lecture given by Smith shortly after taking up his first academic post and provides an excellent insight into his ideas about the relationship between scholarship, knowledge, and Christian faith.

6. "Captain Conder and Modern Critics," *Contemporary Review* 51 (April 1887): 561-62.

remarks on men who were not striving to go forward in their work. Thoroughly conscientious himself, he had a feeling of contempt alike for teachers or students who were not laying out their energy on the task set before them, and he did not hesitate to express it as occasions arose!"[7] This may well relate to Smith's apparent contempt for Principal Rainy, whom he later saw as his adversary and betrayer in his university trial. Lilley's esteem for gentlemanly good manners is totally out of tune with Smith's own restless and impatient quest for knowledge. Yet Lilley is probably correct in relating much of this to Smith's education, which, I believe, provides a key to his unusual character. In an age when college students were, for the most part, recruited from dreary public and church schools where education often followed a routine which eliminated adventure and pleasure from the discovery of new ideas and facts, Smith was educated entirely at home by a father of original and strong character and with an unusual scholarly background in mathematics, classics, Hebrew, and theology. Little time seems to have been wasted in drudge-work, and Smith's own extraordinary gifts were exploited fully but lovingly by his parents. Smith's bond with his father was unusually warm and close, and it is clear that what many fellow students and faculty found unusual and even unsettling in Smith was simply his unmitigated pleasure and love in learning.

Smith's parents maintained that while they set readings and examined their children's work, the children were left to themselves to read and pursue their studies. Not only does this account for Smith's individual approach to scholarship, but it also attests to the enormous drive for achievement instilled by the Smiths in their children. For that family, knowledge and learning were essential to godliness.

Another virtue gained in the Smith household may be viewed as a defect in terms of its failure to provide Smith with the armament to survive in a world governed by such expediencies as deference to public opinion and the political exploitation of ignorance and prejudice, and by that narrow fear of questions shown by all second-rate minds. For Smith arrived in college convinced that all ideas were open to question and that if indeed something were true, then intensive examination would only purify and improve one's understanding of it. To him, controversy and discussion were ameliorative midwives in the deliver-

---

7. Rev. J. P. Lilley, "William Robertson Smith: Recollections of a Fellow Student," *Expositor*, 8th ser., no. 115 (July 1920), p. 126.

ance of truth. It is, of course, true, as Smith himself observed, that "no man is so infallible that his exegesis is not in a measure attracted towards his dogmatic prepossessions and vice versa,"[8] and we find Smith himself responding rather touchily to criticism; [9] yet this hardly dims his general sense of relish and judiciousness in scholarly response and exchange, virtues often remarked upon by most of his colleagues. We shall see that these open and free attitudes eventually led to the overwhelming experience of his life, his trial for heretical or dangerous religious views in 1876–81.

The radical character of Smith's thought is clearly demonstrated in both his readings and works. His sympathies tended to be with reformers and iconoclasts—provided they were well informed and had deep integrity. He admired Luther but disliked the Fathers, especially Augustine; he was more attracted to the study of the prophets than of the priests and the Law, and he preferred the adventurous challenges and perplexities of an ever-changing (and therefore perfecting) biblical criticism to the construction of a formal theology.[10]

Smith is described as short, about five feet, four inches tall, with a slight but sinewy. round-shouldered build. He had a swarthy complexion, with dark hair and eyes. His friend J. S. Black describes him as having somewhat Oriental, "sensual" features. In his earlier portraits he appears a handsome, forceful looking man. He was described by all who knew him as nervous, impetuous, and excitable by temperament. This was reflected in his somewhat rapid stride and in outbreaks of eczema which disfigured his face during periods of emotional tension and overwork. However, the characterization of him as "impetuous" seems somewhat unjust; if it applies to him at all, it would only hold insofar as his personal relations are concerned, for he had little patience with unlearned, pompous persons and no inclination for iridescent and idle chitchat. But he delighted in animated scholarly discussion and debate and was disarmingly well informed on an extraordinarily wide range of topics, hardly surprising in one of the few men who, as editor, had carefully read through the entire *Encyclopaedia Britannica.* Yet Smith disliked polemic for its own sake and tried rather to present contrasting

8. Review in *The Academy* 4 (1873): 369.

9. Letter in *The Academy* 36 (1889): 374–75.

10. Some of Smith's most sensitive insights pertain to the prophets and their language, and it is worthwhile to note that he regarded Luther's interpretation in these areas as an important inspiration for his own analysis (see *LE,* pp. 401–2).

issues in such a way that a just assessment of a problem might be achieved. To him controversy was simply a quick and useful means to understanding. Smith's animated conversation was a source of great pleasure to those equal to exchanging ideas and knowledge with him; if there was a disarming quality in it, this derived from one of Smith's most engaging traits, his spontaneity and candor in revealing unguardedly the course of his own reasoning and speculation. However, Innes suggests that for some Smith's energy and scholarship may have seemed disruptive and tedious: "Substantially the same theory [that the church should change through the influence of progressive individuals]—but with sharper angles and with some suggestions from a modern German school—was put forth in the only sermon I ever heard from Professor Robertson Smith (who had at dinner the previous evening instructed our host, Mr. Campbell of Tullichewan, in agriculture and the management of estates, put me right as to Roman law, and convicted two other gentlemen of obvious ignorance, each upon his own subject—and all after spending the Saturday afternoon in playing tennis like a demon, to the discomfiture of both sexes and every age)."[11]

Unfortunately, Smith's speaking voice, with its thick Scottish burr and sharp, shrill quality, detracted somewhat from his potential as a preacher and lecturer, at least to some who recollect him. Reverend Barry, describing the sermons Smith felt obliged to give before his appointment at Aberdeen, said, "I have been struck with what seemed a tender reverence of tone in his whole service, spite of the natural irreverence of his voice";[12] and Frazer, too, refers to the high, piercing intonation of Smith's voice.[13]

Much has been made of Smith's ill health, but it should be noted that he founded and participated in a gymnastic society while a student at Edinburgh and was most skillful at gymnastic feats, and that he was an able hiker and was later fit to make long desert journeys by camel. Sheer overwork must account in large part for his early death. In his later years he pursued a schedule of reading, research, and academic duties which led him to omit lunch from his schedule and, more often than not, to work far into the night.

11. A. Taylor Innes, *Chapters of Reminiscence* (London: Hodder and Stoughton, 1913), p. 193.

12. *Life,* p. 125.

13. James G. Frazer, *The Gorgon's Head* (London: Macmillan, 1927), p. 278.

In his early student days, Smith appears somewhat puritanical and even harsh in regard to many pleasures in life. Although he enjoyed poetry and literature, he found Goethe "lacking in moral tone" and had to force himself to read a novel each Christmas vacation as a duty in broadening his outlook. He appears to have been utterly devoid of appreciation of Western music, and yet he showed remarkable sensitivity in tone and rhythm in declaiming Arabic and Hebrew poetry. In his later years, his manners became far more worldly and he gained some reputation not only as a witty and charming conversationalist at high-table dinners at college and clubs, but as a knowing judge of fine wines and good tobaccos. At his death, he is said to have had an admirable collection not only of rare books but of fine Oriental rugs and good paintings and prints.

Despite his enormous drive for work, it is clear that Smith was kind and generous in his relations with serious students and dedicated researchers. His own work was frequently and extensively curtailed by many days of reading and annotating manuscripts and proofs of other scholars and in the exchange of a voluminous scholarly correspondence. In his role as editor of the *Encyclopaedia Britannica,* in his many ties with learned societies and scholars on the Continent, and his legendary command of foreign languages—he is said to have spoken perfect German and Arabic, to have written superb Latin, and to have had good knowledge of Dutch, French, Greek, Hebrew, and assorted other European and Near Eastern languages—Smith, perhaps more than any other contemporary in Britain, provided a tie between the scholars of Britain and those of the Continent. His diffuse and always current connections with foreign scholars were considered, during his time, as one of the greatest assets he provided his college and university. It is no exaggeration to say that Smith's editorial responsibilities led him to have personal acquaintance with nearly every important intellectual in Britain and a large number on the Continent, not only Semitic and biblical scholars, but physicists, mathematicians, philosophers, historians, and biologists, men as different as Swinburne and Darwin, Huxley and Kelvin, Spencer and Burne-Jones.

If one may single out a fault in Smith, it is his almost obsessive scrupulousness toward perfection, whether he was preparing a tutorial for a student or an article for publication or merely proofreading a colleague's rough draft of a paper. Such intensive devotion to thoroughness and detail, with little sense of proportion, by general consensus of his friends and colleagues, greatly contributed to a dissipation of his energies. Smith worked up until the final days of his illness, despite intense physical pain. He seems to have taken the fatal diagnosis (apparently tuberculosis of the spinal column) with stoic reserve, although he bitterly regretted not being able to complete his researches and feared the pain his death might cause his family. Indeed, the deaths of his two brothers, his sister, and his father appear to have led him to accept the prospect of a premature death. In any case, from all accounts he seems to have made an effort to shield others from any embarrassment or discomfort over his own sufferings.

The Libel (Heresy) Case

During the period of his stay at Edinburgh and Aberdeen, Smith made frequent visits to the Continent and engaged in a wide correspondence with scholars there and elsewhere. His unusual familiarity with current international research in biblical and Semitic studies led to his being selected as a consultant for essays in the forthcoming ninth edition of the *Encyclopaedia Britannica,* published by a Scottish firm and very much dominated by Scots intellectuals. Smith was chosen because it was felt by the publisher and especially by the series' new, progressive editor, Professor Thomas Spencer Baynes, that biblical entries in the *Encyclopaedia* should reflect "the new criticism," and Smith's own manifold connections with such scholars were unrivalled in Britain. This was well appreciated since, during this time, Smith provided a regular review and digest in the *British and Foreign Evangelical Review,* published in Edinburgh, in which he covered new works written in German, Dutch, and French and which were often unlikely to be otherwise noted by his less cosmopolitan colleagues. In 1875 Smith was chosen for membership on the Committee for Revision of the Authorized Version of the Bible, an extraordinary distinction for a scholar of twenty-nine. In that same year the first of Smith's essays for the *Encyclopaedia* appeared: "Angel" and then "Bible." Neither expressed views different from those Smith had already presented in college lectures and scholarly articles over the previous five years; nor were these views in any way appreciably different from the generally accepted views of other contemporary biblical and Semitic scholars. By today's standards, they were conventional indeed.[14] Yet these articles led to one of the most famous academic disputes in Victorian Britain, and to Smith's removal from the college. To understand how two such apparently unexceptionable essays could have had such an exaggerated impact, we must consider two important and interesting factors: the temper and structure of the Free Church of Scotland at this time and the character of Smith. The "Robertson Smith affair," as this was sometimes termed, was regarded by Smith as the most important event in his life and remained a source of bitterness to him until his death, despite the enormous respect and esteem he later attained both in Britain and abroad. Consequently, these events merit some analysis as a kind of social drama which provides insight into how Smith saw himself and his work and how he was evaluated in his time.

Smith's professorship was at the Free Church Divinity College, which had been attached to the University of Aberdeen in 1850. He had been ordained as a minister in the Free Church and was expected to convey its tenets to young aspirant ministers under his instruction. As a result, his views were seen by many as pertinent far beyond the realm of scholarship, for he could affect every parish to which his students were later sent as ministers. This was significant, for it was mainly over the issue of whether the ordinary parishioners could control the type of ministers they would receive that the Free Church had in 1843 split from the main body. Many in the Free Church even claimed themselves not to be a splinter group at all but to be the only branch of the National Church of Scotland which had continued to adhere to its original beliefs set out at its foundation in 1560. The Free Church termed itself "free" as opposed to "established" in that it held itself to be free from the abuses of the heads of the church to infringe upon the rights of local congregations. The central issue of the Free Church's foundation had been whether the heads of the church could force a congregation to accept a minister whom the local group disliked but whom the heads of the church had chosen and endorsed.

In the 1870s some of the difficulties within the Free Church were a reflection of the social problems which disturbed much of Victorian

---

14. For example, see Georg Fohrer, *Introduction to the Old Testament* (London: Society for Promoting Christian Knowledge, 1970).

Scotland.[15] Industrialization and trade favored the Lowland merchants and workers and the Lowland towns, where there was a quickening and broadening of social life and thought, while the Highlands remained economically poor and relatively unchanged. Indeed, the Highlanders reacted hostilely to most attempts at change, which they interpreted as further threats to their stability and integrity. The Highland members of the Free Church were overrepresented in the Church Assembly. The products of a bitter schism only thirty years before, the Free Churchmen were intensely sensitive to the potential danger of splits within their body, and therefore moderate and liberal churchmen tended to yield to the demands of Highland conservatives in order to prevent yet another division. In such a situation, cautious but informed and politically "wise" liberals tended to balk at confrontation with fundamentalists and preferred to keep issues somewhat vague, while ambitious demagogues could appeal to the conventional wisdom of the uninformed, encouraging attacks against those who sought modification of unquestioned tradition, especially when this could be associated with any foreign influences.

Faced with such potential conflicts, the most powerful leaders of the Free Church sought to avoid all situations of formal confrontation between the two social and ideological poles within the church. It was clearly hoped that so long as divergent beliefs and conduct were pursued discretely and quietly, considerable leeway could be tolerated within the church. It was for these reasons that some of the more enlightened church leaders, even while privately conceding the scholarly correctness of Smith's opinions, viewed him with alarm and hoped to see such a troublemaker removed from any prominent position in the church. Smith met his critics with demands for public confrontation and with barrages of articles, letters, pamphlets and public lectures. Smith's integrity—or pride—served as a catalyst for a wide range of divisions, involving persons essentially unaware of the technicalities of the scholarly issues involved.

The two *Encyclopaedia* articles by Smith at first attracted little attention, since they appeared in volumes not readily accessible (physi-

---

15. See Donald Carswell, *Brother Scots* (New York: Harcourt, Brace, 1928); for a useful contemporary account of the Free Church by Smith's friend and biographer, J. S. Black, see "Free Church of Scotland," *EB* 9: 742–46.

cally or economically) to most people, especially those most likely to be upset by them. Furthermore, they were written in a highly technical and condensed style. As one defender of Smith wrote: "The subjects handled in the articles were comparatively novel—to professional readers—and being clothed in language demanding attention, accuracy of thought, previous knowledge of recondite discussions and learned references, is it at all wonderful that much gross exaggeration should take place, and that even persons of receptive and reasonable minds should be hurried into a summary condemnation of the author's views, without having any surer ground to stand upon than the general *on dit* of others little better informed than themselves?"[16] However, the *Edinburgh Courant* sent the second volume of the *Encyclopaedia,* containing "Angel" and "Bible," for review to Dr. A. H. Charteris, professor of biblical criticism at Edinburgh University. Charteris was a very conservative churchman who violently attacked Smith's articles as undermining Christian faith. Smith, as was his nature, wrote a rejoining letter to the *Daily Review* (21 June 1876). Unfortunately, the issue was then taken up by the Reverend James Begg, a preacher in the Free Church well known for his histrionic preaching and reactionary views, exactly the type of person able and likely to stir up popular disruption within the Free Church.[17]

It is useful at this point to review what Smith wrote as well as to indicate in what ways this was viewed as questionable by some members

16.   Anonymous [Benjamin Bell], *Thoughts on the Aberdeen Case by a Pre-Disruption Elder* (Edinburgh: I. Maclaren, 1880), p. 6.

17.   Carswell, *Brother Scots,* presents a fairly balanced account of the dispute. Smith wrote various letters and pamphlets explaining his position. The Free Church's view is presented in *The Libel against Professor William Robertson Smith: Report of Proceedings into the Free Church Presbytery of Aberdeen, Feb. 14, to March 14, 1878, with Form of Libel* (Aberdeen: Murray; Edinburgh: Maclaren and Macniven; Glasgow: D. Bryce, 1878). Presumably another useful source of information is the Free Church's *Reports and Sketches of the General Assembly of 1880* (not obtained). There is a very extensive polemical literature in response to Smith's biblical articles in the *EB* and to his subsequent trial. The overwhelming majority of these pamphlets are directed against Smith, primarily by the more fundamentalist and unscholarly elements of the Free Church. In contrast, the reports, editorials, and letters published by the contemporary press are more evenly divided in the views expressed; indeed, the secular press tended to support Smith as a martyr to those social aspects of Scotland which were least favorable to change. I have not drawn directly here on most of this material since its volume is out of all proportion to its significance for understanding Smith's career. However, since little of it has been cited elsewhere, I have listed Smith's tracts and the writings of his opponents in the Bibliography in the hope that this may aid other scholars.

of the Free Church. The original formal charges against Smith were eight, the first seven based on the article "Bible" and the last based on "Angel." These were later revised, but the basic issues are clear enough in the first version of the charges. These were heard before the church in the form of a libel action rather than heresy, although, for the purposes of Smith's career in the church, the results were the same. It was claimed by Smith's accusers that he had stated that: (1) Levitical laws were not instituted at the time of Moses; (2) Deuteronomy was not simply a reflection of historical facts, nor was it all written during the time of Moses; (3) sacred writers took liberties and made errors of transcription just like other historical authors and scribes;[18] (4) certain of the scriptures were a kind of fiction or allegory and not literally true, even though they did reflect certain "truths"; (5) that the Songs of Solomon were probably a political and social satire and quite devoid of spiritual significance;[19] (6) that the fact that New Testament authors cite passages from the Old Testament in no way can assure us that those Old Testament passages are thereby beyond question, emendation or correction; (7) prophetic predictions were often due to spiritual insights and not always to direct supernatural revelations; and (8) the reality of angels is a matter of assumption rather than direct and explicit biblical teaching.

In a sense, all of these charges are essentially what Smith contended, but Smith and most competent biblical scholars of that day (and now) would have contended that such interpretations are nearly uncontrovertible, and yet that they hardly diminish the deeper and clearer meanings of the Bible. Indeed, Smith argued that: "To the indolent theologian the necessity of distinguishing between these quasi-historical precedents, which were meant to be taken only as laws, and the actual history, which was meant to be taken literally, is naturally unwelcome; but to the diligent and reverent student, it affords the keys for the solution of many difficulties, and the natural removal of contradictions, which, on the current exegesis, present a constant stumbling block to faith."[20]

The assertions of Smith's attackers were oversimplified and crude in comparison with Smith's own statements, but some irrelevant issues

18.   A point Smith elaborates in "Chronicles," *EB* 5 (1876): 706-9.
19.   Smith expands this later in "Canticles," *EB* 5 (1876): 32-36.
20.   *The Old Testament in the Jewish Church*, p. 387.

were also raised by his critics which clearly did Smith no good in the long run. His enemies even went so far as to present Smith as a purveyor of insidious foreign influences undermining hearty and healthy Scottish faith.

Smith's own views were clearly and firmly presented at a lecture given at the Free Church Divinity College the same academic year that his troubles began:

Is the Bible really such a book that its worth for the Church is undermined when its history and ideas are examined by the aid of the very methods of historical and literary criticism which have shed a flood of light on every other part of ancient history and ancient literature?[21]

The Spirit of God works in and through human nature, and so the relation of the redeemed to God becomes a genuine element in history, of which historical science is bound to take cognisance, and which is as capable of historical appreciation as any other psychological element in the annals of our race. Accordingly modern theological science is altogether right, when it insists that the Bible must be studied by the aid of the same principle of historical continuity which is employed in the examination of other records of the past.[22]

The Bible and the Bible history were still too exclusively looked at from the supernatural point of view. Now the evolution of God's dealings with man cannot be understood, except by looking at the human side of the process. The only idea of moral and spiritual evolution possible to us, is that of evolution in accordance with psychological laws. The nexus sought must always be psychological. The teleology of revelation is divine; but the pragmatism of the revealing history must be human.[23]

What the biblical science can do to throw a fuller light on the plan of redemption is simply to reconstruct, by the ordinary methods of historical-psychological combination, the human complement of the divine manifestation. But if we can trace the process of the Old Testament religion completely from the side of psychology and human history, the divine elements in the process will take their proper place of themselves, unless with arbitrary rationalism we forcibly thrust them aside. For it is the postulate of all moral religion, that God commu-

21. "The Progress of Old Testament Studies," p. 486.
22. Ibid., p. 488.
23. Ibid., p. 489.

nicates himself to man in such a way that his revelation is interwoven with history, without violence or breach of psychological laws.[24]

A committee of the church unofficially communicated its disapproval of these *Encyclopaedia* essays both to Smith and to his superiors at the college. The principal, Dr. Robert Rainy,[25] wanted Smith to retract his published views. Instead, Smith reaffirmed his faith in Christianity but also his conviction that his essays represented a truer and clearer reading of the Bible. A flood of pamphlets and speeches appeared, chiefly against Smith and reaffirming a literal interpretation of the Bible. Popular local demagogues such as Reverend Beggs, Reverend George Macauley, and Reverend Sir Henry Moncreiff, demanded Smith's removal. The more cautious and temperate members of the church sought to prevent any public and formal confrontation between Smith and his critics, fearing yet another schism. But Smith demanded a formal accusation and the right to confront his critics. In 1877 Smith was suspended from the college at his own request. He published two booklets replying to each point in the charges.[26] During this period Smith toured Glasgow, Edinburgh, and elsewhere, giving public addresses explaining the bases for his views and the nature of the "higher criticism." These lectures were later expanded and published as *The Old Testament in the Jewish Church* and *The Prophets of Israel.* In the hearings of the Church Assembly which followed in 1878, Smith succeeded in having the charges discussed point by point. As a result of Smith's superior intelligence, wit, and eloquence, the original set of accusations were dropped. However, the case was still considered unsettled, and a new set of charges was set before the General Assembly. These involved the specific issue raised by Smith's interpretation of the authorship and dates of Deuteronomy and, more vaguely, the general

24. Ibid.

25. Most accounts favorable to Smith view Rainy critically. In his own day he was considered a progressive liberal in religious and other matters. Rainy was intent on preventing further divisions within the Free Church and was by temperament ill-disposed to controversy. I was unable to secure Carnegie Simpson, *Life of Rainy* (London: Hodder and Stoughton, 1909), but did secure A. Taylor Innes, *Chapters of Reminiscence,* in which there is a biographical sketch of Rainy, including comment on his attitude toward Smith (pp. 179-258).

26. *Answer to the Form of Libel now before the Free Church Presbytery of Aberdeen* (1878); *Additional Answer to the Libel, with some Account of the Evidence* (1878).

issue that his teachings might cause serious weakening of faith among believers, especially those unable to judge scholarly and technical issues. It is ironic that the latter charge ran counter both to the original precepts of the Free Church and to Smith's view of scholarship; the General Assembly had framed its accusations in a manner that implied that a select group of churchmen could and should judge for the church and rejected the notion that each believer and each congregation could come to its own views regarding such issues. This was clearly against traditional principles strongly held by many members of the Free Church.

By this time, Smith had spent a year in turmoil with no clear resolution of his difficulties. In early November 1878 he left for Egypt to improve his Arabic. He also took the opportunity to travel in Syria and Palestine. In the late spring of the following year he returned to Scotland to prepare for the final hearings of his case. To many it now seemed a distinct possibility that Smith might consider leaving his post, because he was tired and embittered over the entire affair, and because he could accomplish far more useful things outside the stultifying atmosphere of Aberdeen. He did indeed try, unsuccessfully, to secure a chair in mathematics at the University of Glasgow. Depressed, he set out on another sojourn to the Middle East in November 1879. He stayed abroad nearly six months, spending most of his time in Cairo and Alexandria, but making excursions into the Libyan desert and the Hejaz, and an eleven day trip to the Fayum and the Nitrian Lakes with Richard Burton.[27] At this time he was invited to take a chair of Hebrew at Harvard, but he declined. He left Alexandria in April 1880, and after a visit with McLennan in Italy, arrived for the General Assembly hearing of his case in late May.

The assembly had decided to admonish him for having been careless, but for no more, and it had agreed to reinstate him to his chair. However, in early June 1880, two scholarly essays by Smith appeared which settled his fate with the Free Church — his essay on animal worship, which had been inspired by McLennan, and his essay on the Hebrew language.[28] These were seen not only as sure proof that Smith

27.   Burton's few comments on the trip appear in a series of letters written to Lord Granville. See Isabel Burton, *The Life of Captain Sir Richd. F. Burton, K.C.M.G., F.R.G.S.* (London: Chapman and Hall, 1893), 2: 192-201.

28.   "Animal Tribes in the Old Testament," *Journal of Philology* 9 (1880): 75-100;

was unlikely to subside into conformity but that his scholarly researches would lead him into ever more serious and threatening confrontations with his more conservative fellow churchmen. Furthermore, Smith had given his assurances at the earlier hearings that he would refrain from publishing any disturbing articles in the future and that he would clear any such questionable work with his fellows. The essays in question had been submitted before such promises had been made, and their publication was delayed due to a series of difficulties with publishers. However, it should be clear from what we know of Smith's character that such assurances, however sincerely given, were totally at odds with Smith's own nature and could never have long been kept. Smith was incapable of either silence or inactivity regarding the quest for knowledge and understanding, regardless of the consequences to himself. Nonetheless, it is clear that Smith himself had thought that he had indeed lived up to his part of the agreement, for he had declined to write the essays on Isaiah and Israel requested of him by the *Encyclopaedia,* even though these were topics of intense interest to him.

During the height of these difficulties Smith was again offered a post at Harvard, which he again refused. Despite his growing scholarly reputation elsewhere, however, in Aberdeen and Edinburgh the public outcry against the Hebrew language essay was predictable, given the earlier reaction to the Bible essay. The General Assembly's reaction to the animal worship paper was even stronger: "First, concerning marriage and the marriage laws in Israel, the views expressed are so gross and so fitted to pollute the moral sentiments of the community that they cannot be considerd except within the closed doors of any court of this Church. Secondly, concerning animal worship in Israel, the views expressed by the Professor are not only contrary to the facts recorded and the statements made in Holy Scripture, but they are gross and sensual — fitted to pollute and debase public sentiment."[29]

Smith, meanwhile, remained suspended from his professorship. Shortly after, *The Old Testament in the Jewish Church* was published and received very favorable reviews. This contained the first published

---

"Hebrew Language and Literature," *EB* 11 (1880): 594-602. Stanley Cook describes the first paper as a turning point in biblical studies, since this is the first application of anthropological research to Old Testament criticism (Review, *Hibbert Journal* 10 [1912]: 213).

29. Report by the Commission of the Assembly, in *Life,* pp. 381-82.

version of Smith's new theory of sacrifice which he was later to develop in his classic book on Semitic religion. On 26 May 1881 Smith was formally removed from his professorship.

Despite his official disgrace within the Free Church College, Smith emerged from his ordeal a figure of new fame and prestige, honored internationally for his scholarship and supported locally by those who saw him as a symbol of the opposition to the reactionary forces enervating much of Scottish life. In a long and angry editorial, *The Glasgow Herald* (25 May 1881) condemned the bigoted and witch-hunting conduct of the Reverend Begg and the Reverend Moncreiff and the opportunistic and apparently cynical conduct of Principal Rainy. "This remarkable and dangerous position Dr. Rainy has maintained for the last two years, and it is not surprising to find him before the Assembly met preparing a scheme to barke inquiry, and sacrifice Professor Robertson Smith, not upon the altar of orthodoxy, but in the shambles of expediency." "Professor Robertson Smith's criticism is constructive, informing, homogeneous, and logical. It is a system which many Free Churchmen have gladly adopted, and its method has been received as the true method by very many more. What does Dr. Rainy oppose to it? Dr. Begg's position is clear in its unintellectual doggedness." It concludes by describing the final outcome of the case as "Dr. Rainy's chaos of the formless 'unsafe,' and of the shapeless 'tendency.' "[30]

Smith's Later Career

Smith suddenly had found himself without a post through which he could direct his energies. More serious, he found himself with few savings and only a meager income from his writings. Although some of his friends urged him to take the college to court to secure some of his salary, Smith refused. Instead, through the influence of friends, he was offered a full-time editorial post with the *Encyclopaedia Britannica,* becoming coeditor with Professor Spencer Baynes, and on Baynes's death, sole editor.[31] He moved to Edinburgh where the *Encyclopaedia's*

30. The bitterness persisted even after Smith's death; in 1896 an attack on "the new criticism" was published which was so hostile to Smith that he was never mentioned by name but simply referred to as "the late editor of the *Encyclopaedia Britannica*.". This attack was endorsed by the Assyriologist, A. H. Sayce, and also by Gladstone and by various members of the Church of Scotland. See W. L. Baxter, *Sanctuary and Sacrifice: A Reply to Wellhausen* (London: Eyre and Spottiswoode, 1896).

31. For useful discussions of Smith's work with the *Encyclopaedia,* see Herman Kogan,

publishers, A. and C. Black (also his publishers) had their offices. He had grown to prefer Edinburgh to Aberdeen in any case due to its more stimulating intellectual and social life. There he was elected to the Athenaeum and pursued a wide international scholarly correspondence. Despite his past difficulties, he remained on good terms with many members of the Free Church and was even nominated to the presbytery of Edinburgh. (Contrary to the implications of some of the accounts of his life, he was never forced out of the Free Church.) Whereas Smith had written less than twenty essays in the first eleven volumes of the *Encyclopaedia,* he wrote over two hundred for the remaining thirteen volumes. In April 1882, while at Edinburgh, he published *The Prophets of Israel.*

On 1 January 1883, Smith was appointed Lord Almoner Reader in Arabic at Cambridge, succeeding Professor E. H. Palmer, who had been murdered in the Sinai the previous October.[32] The post paid £ 50 a year and required only one annual lecture; since Smith had little money, he remained in Edinburgh with the *Encyclopaedia* until October, when he was made a member of Trinity College, Cambridge. At Christmas of that year he moved into college quarters. Smith's Cambridge appointment was in large measure due to the influence of Professor William Wright, Adams Professor of Arabic, whom Smith had first met through their common work on the Old Testament Revision Committee.

At Cambridge, Smith gave a series of lectures on pre-Islamic Arab history, a topic he often claimed as his favorite. He also made various scholarly visits to the Continent and continued editing the *Encyclopaedia.* In January 1885, Smith was elected a Fellow of Christ's College, Cambridge, which was to be his home for the remainder of his life. Upon taking up residence at Christ's, Smith relinquished some of his responsibilities for the *Encyclopaedia,* but remained editor-in-chief; for Smith, this still meant that he felt compelled to read every article submitted, to provide careful advisement on the selection of contributors, and to prepare many articles himself. During his first year at Christ's, he published *Kinship and Marriage in Early Arabia,* one of his

---

The Great EB: The Story of the Encyclopaedia Britannica (Chicago: University of Chicago Press, 1958), pp. 172-78; and Anonymous, *Adam and Charles Black 1807-1957* (London: A. and C. Black, 1957), esp. pp. 35-49.

32. See [Smith] (unsigned), "Palmer, Edward Henry," *EB* 18 (1885): 192.

finest achievements and the model for all subsequent analyses of aceph-
alous, segmentary systems of descent and social organization.[33] Ironically, the weakest sections of Smith's studies such as this are those
inspired by his friend McLennan's theories regarding the evolution of
kinship organization and marriage and their relation to totemism. Yet it
was these sections which attracted particularly strong enthusiasm during Smith's day, including supplementary studies by the Dutch scholar
Wilken, the German scholars Wellhausen and Nöldeke, and the Hun-
garian Goldziher. It was Smith, above all, who led the popularization of
McLennan's notions about totemism and who encouraged his own
protegé, Sir James Frazer, to write a pioneer survey essay on the topic in
the *Encyclopaedia*[34] Smith himself wrote to the *Encyclopaedia* publishers: "I hope that Messrs. Black clearly understand that Totemism is a
subject of growing importance, daily mentioned in magazines and
papers, but of which there is no good account anywhere — precisely one
of those cases where we have an opportunity of being ahead of everyone
and getting some reputation. There is no article in the volume for which
I am more solicitous. I have taken much personal pains with it,
guiding Frazer carefully in his treatment; and he has put about seven
months' hard work on it to make it the standard article on the subject.
We must make room for it, whatever else goes."[35]

In February 1886 Henry Bradshaw, the librarian for the University of
Cambridge, died, and Smith was chosen to be his successor. This
involved a considerable increase in Smith's income but an enormous
amount of additional work, especially for someone as conscientious as
Smith. Smith supervised the construction of an addition to the library,
the Hancock Building, and a major revision in cataloguing methods.As
usual, Smith carried out his work unaided, for he had little faith in
cooperative administration, in contrast to his strong convictions about
cooperation in scholarly endeavor. He is quoted as having said, "I am
quite sure any one of the Syndicate could draw up an abler report than

---

33. For two contrasting evaluations of Smith's achievement, see E. Peters, Preface to *Kinship and Marriage in Early Arabia* (Boston: Beacon paperback, 1967); T. O. Beidel-man, review of preceding, *Anthropos* 63-64 (1968-69): 592-95.

34. James G. Frazer, "Totemism," *EB* 18 (1888): 467-76; Smith also appears to have persuaded his publishers to print Frazer's first essay on the topic, *Totemism* (Edinburgh: A. and C. Black, 1887).

35. *Life*, p. 494.

this, but I am quite sure that all of the Syndicate working together cannot."[36] The library, the editorship of the *Encyclopaedia* (even though J. S. Black had in fact taken over many of the administrative duties), teaching, and his writing—all of this imposed a very heavy burden upon Smith. But this was not all: he also served the university on the Oriental Board of Studies, the Press Syndicate, and the Library Syndicate. And added to this was the loss of his youngest brother, Herbert, who died of tuberculosis at the end of 1877, and the need to make special arrangements for the care of his father, who was suffering from declining health.

Despite this heavy work load, which was making visible inroads on his health, in April 1887 Smith accepted an invitation from the Burnett Trustees to deliver a series of lectures on Semitic religion. These were to consist of twelve lectures over a five-year period. It was arranged that these would be given in the Hall of Marischal College, University of Aberdeen, and that they would cover the very topic which had led to his leaving that city and university. This same period, the close of 1888, marked the completion of the ninth edition of the *Encyclopaedia Britannica* which Smith celebrated with a gala dinner for British and foreign dignitaries held at the Hall of Christ's College, Cambridge.

Smith's editorship of the ninth edition would in itself justify him a permanent place in British intellectual history, for that edition stands unique in the history of the *Encyclopaedia,* in large part a reflection of Smith's and Baynes's progressive and expanded view of scholarship and relevance. The ninth has been called the "scholars' encyclopaedia" both because it contains essays by an exceedingly distinguished international set of scholars and because it is the first to incorporate the profound intellectual advances made in nearly all fields of nineteenth-century scholarship. Furthermore, this was the first edition of a major encyclopaedia to be circulated on a mass international basis. The distribution rights to the *Encyclopaedia* were taken up by Americans as well and, through the support of the London *Times,* a cheap, installment-purchase version of the edition was made available to a public unable to afford the earlier versions. In short, Smith's achievement made a great impact upon the popularly educated thousands as well as upon scholars.

The first set of Burnett Lectures were delivered in October 1888 and March 1889. Shortly after delivering the last of these, Smith left for a

36. Ibid., p. 490.

tour of Algeria and Tunisia. On his return in the late spring, he found his friend Professor William Wright dying. Wright was holder of the Sir Thomas Adams Chair in Arabic at Cambridge, and Smith succeeded him. That November, Smith published the first series of his Burnett Lectures, *Lectures on the Religion of the Semites*. In general, the book was most warmly received as a major achievement of scholarship and original analysis; it was considered the finest of Smith's published works. The year 1889 marked the highpoint in Smith's success and sense of accomplishment and was followed by uninterrupted personal misfortune. In January 1890 Smith became seriously ill and underwent surgery; in February his father died. Although still unwell, Smith gave the second series of Burnett Lectures that March. After vacationing in Egypt, he gave the third series of lectures in December 1891. Apparently, almost no record of these second and third series of lectures survives other than a few notes by Smith, reportedly found among his papers examined by his biographers, Black and Chrystal.[37] The following years saw a rapid decline in Smith's health accompanied by considerable physical pain. No medical aid or prolonged vacation in the sun seemed to help. To the end, Smith worked on revisions for a new edition of *The Old Testament in the Jewish Church* and, most important of all to him, a greatly revised second edition of the *Lectures*.[38] He continued teaching students from his sickbed at the college and worked until two weeks before his death correcting proofs of the religion book. He died on 31 March 1894, age forty-eight, and was buried in Keig churchyard with the rest of the family.

37. The editors of the *Encyclopaedia Biblica* remark that some of the contributors to it — presumably Cheyne, among others, since he appears to have had access to Smith's papers — have provided some quotes from the manuscripts of the second and third sets of lectures regarding the topics of priesthood, divination, prophecy, Semitic polytheism, and cosmogony. See *EBL* 1: xi (Introduction by T. K. Cheyne and J. S. Black, eds.).

38. Frazer seems to imply that at least one of the deletions and changes in this edition reflects a concern that Smith's earlier edition might have discredited the teachings of the New Testament (Frazer, *The Gorgon's Head*, p. 289). This is clearly the view taken by Evans-Pritchard (*Theories of Primitive Religion* [Oxford: Clarendon Press, 1965], p. 52). There is little in Smith's writings to suggest that he was likely to have made changes for any reason other than securing what he believed to be more precise scholarship. At no time did Smith seem to doubt that scholarly findings would do other than better delineate the true message of the Bible. Nor does it seem likely that Smith's publishers or his literary executors made such alterations posthumously since they had shown themselves consistently supportive of Smith's strong views. The reviews of the first edition provided some criticism on ethnological grounds and on the question of Smith's perspective of the overall

Smith's Field Experience

Unlike most of his compeers and indeed unlike most of his immediate successors in anthropology, Smith actually saw the lands about which he wrote. As has been noted above, in 1878–79 he spent about six months in the Middle East, mainly in Cairo, where he worked on his spoken Arabic, but also toured Palestine and Syria. In the fall of 1879 he spent another six months in the Middle East, again mainly in Cairo and Alexandria, but also making a two month inland tour of the Arabian Peninsula, a visit to the Libyan desert, and an excursion into the Fayum and Nitrian Lakes with Richard Burton. In the spring of 1889 Smith made a brief tour of Algeria and Tunisia, including some of the inland oases. His final visit was a winter cruise to Egypt in 1890.

Smith deeply enjoyed his visits to the Middle East. It was clearly not only a matter of improving his languages; it was also that the life there appealed to him. It is said that he delighted in wandering about the old cities, and it is clear from his descriptions that he was a shrewd observer. Smith traveled in native garb, and mainly by camel. With his swarthy looks and dark hair and beard, he looked as Arabic as the most famous arabophile and Arab-poser of them all, his temporary comrade, Richard Burton. Smith appears tolerant, even easy-going in the day to day crises of foreign travel in Victorian times. He reports useful information on local etiquette, housing, diet, and dress. But like so many other Victorians, he remained profoundly pleased with his Britishness. In one

scene of Semitic studies, but after his conflict with the Free Church in the 1880s, the theological implications of Smith's work did not seem to pose serious inhibitions to his assertions. Nevertheless, the deleted passage which Frazer quotes does most clearly associate totemic-like necrophagy with Christ's death and the eucharist. It may be that while this would stir few sophisticated divines today, it may have seriously upset more in Smith's time. The reason for this deletion must remain obscure until Smith's papers and correspondence are available. The passage which Frazer brings to question is provided in the following discussion of Smith's views of sacrifice. The reasons for expunging the passage in question remain unclear, but suggestions of expediency or pusillanimity on the part of either Smith or his publishers require more substantiation than has so far been provided. In examining the differences between the first and second editions, I have found a great many changes, most simply stylistic or else added comment for a polemical point. In a few cases, Smith does remove or add considerable material, usually to correct an extreme view which he had since modified: for example, in lecture I in his discussion of the Unity and Homogeneity of the Semitic Race, or in lecture III in Original Sense of Baal's Land and The Baalim as Lords of Water and Givers of Fertility. However, even in these sections where extensive change and addition of material are involved, all of the basic arguments of Smith remain unaltered in their direction.

unfortunate passage, Smith's enthusiasm for "pure" Arabs and his apparent dislike of Blacks remind one of Burton's more usual excesses of prejudice: "So within Arabia the mixed populations of the towns and the coast, with their large element of negro blood, are far more fanatical than the true unmixed Bedouin stems."[39] Smith's most influential works follow his visits to the Middle East. Though he did not actually live with Arabs, he could and did converse with them (he is said to have spoken superb Arabic, far better than Burton's) and he saw the countryside.

Even so, Smith fell into the use of unfortunate stereotypes when considering the thought processes of alien peoples: "Savages, we know, are not only incapable of separating in thought between phenomenal and noumenal existence, but habitually ignore the distinctions, which to us seem obvious, between organic and inorganic nature, or within the former region between animals and plants, arguing altogether by analogy, and concluding from the known to the unknown with the freedom of men who do not know the difference between the imagination and the reason, they ascribe to all material objects a life analogous to that which their own self-consciousness reveals to them."[40] Smith even gave one of the reasons for mother-right among the early Semites as their sensuality.[41]

While none of the Victorian anthropologists could be said to have done fieldwork in the proper modern sense, a few, like Morgan, Maine, and Smith, did have more than passing encounters with alien, exotic societies. In this, Smith contrasts with Durkheim, Mauss, Frazer, Tylor, Lévy-Bruhl, Marett, and others who readily wrote about alien peoples but who were unable or uninterested in encountering them in the flesh.

THE *LECTURES ON THE RELIGION OF THE SEMITES*

A book may be considered a classic for several reasons, and Smith's *Lectures on the Religion of the Semites* qualifies on at least three counts. First, it is a book that characterizes an important era in the development of social thought. The questions which Smith asks and the answers with which he supports his arguments tell us much about how

39. *LE,* p. 492.
40. *LRS,* pp. 85-86.
41. Ibid., pp. 58-59.

our Victorian predecessors saw the world. The nineteenth century fathered current anthropological thought, and no clear view of contemporary anthropology can neglect an appraisal of the strengths and weaknesses of our Victorian founding fathers.

Second, several particular theories presented in the *Lectures* had profound influence on the work of those who came after him. His work influenced a wide range of anthropologists, sociologists, psychologists, and theologians. However, even if only two such men were to be considered, Durkheim and Freud, these are of such stature that their use of Smith's theories would count as sufficient reason for our trying to appreciate and reevaluate Smith's work.

Third, certain works, even when wrong, raise questions of such basic and perennial importance that an appraisal of these works allows us to take stock of what are the proper tasks and procedures in our field. Smith sought to define the essential nature of religious behavior and approached the analysis of social institutions through comparative and historical studies. However much he may have failed in his task, the problem remains central to social anthropology, and the general methods by which he sought to clarify it are still employed today.

Smith's work is exemplified by a few prevailing concepts. Before examining them in detail, it may be helpful to summarize them briefly.

1. Smith was convinced of the evolutionary progress of both society and, more important, the intellectual consciousness that was both a cause and result of that changing social environment. Nearly all of his writings were cast in some developmental form, whether it was a report of the increasing refinement and progress of biblical scholarship or an account of the evolution of ancient Semitic kinship organization. It is a commonplace today to discuss Victorian notions about evolution and progress in terms of the ideas growing out of the eighteenth-century Enlightenment, the Victorian revolution and its disruptions, and the European confrontation with alien societies in terms of economic and political colonialism. Man's cultural diversity had become ever more apparent, and this presented Europeans with a serious challenge to their notions of what was possible and desirable in society. One way to mitigate the implications of these diversities was to place these alien societies on lower rungs of an evolutionary ladder. While all of the preceding explanations have merit, the influence of Christianity has generally been neglected as a factor behind these evolutionary

trends. Yet Western historical consciousness is rooted deeply in the Judeo-Christian belief in an ethical and intellectual development of a chosen people culminating in the message of Christ. In this sense, Old Testament studies, particulary for the Christian believer, encouraged an evolutionary approach.

2. Smith emphasized the close relation between the nature of social groups and the state of intellectual and moral life. Coupled with his predisposition toward evolutionism, this led Smith toward highly sophisticated perceptions about social process, the nature of social innovation, and cultural relativism.

3. Smith's conception of critical methodology, as learned through the new Continental biblical criticism, led to a mode of analysis and an awareness of social context in studying thought and morality which were consistent with much of the best in modern historical and anthropological research. Smith exemplifies important similarities between the disciplines of historical criticism and anthropological research, a point later fully appreciated by Evans-Pritchard.

4. Smith insisted upon the analytical primacy of ritual (social action) over mythology (belief), a view unfortunately neglected by many of his admirers, including Frazer.

5. Smith believed that the traditions of civilized cultures could be better understood through comparative, evolutionary studies of simpler and presumably earlier cultures. This was his view whether he considered a sociological analysis of marriage or of a religious belief manifested in the Bible.

6. Smith's warm friendship with McLennan led to his persistent championing of two of McLennan's favorite views, the conviction that mother-right invariably preceded father-right as a mode of reckoning descent, and the belief that totemism was a phase of religious belief through which all societies passed. Arguments to support both of these contentions often made use of the typically Victorian doctrine of survivals.

7. Finally, Smith emphasized the rational and ethical aspects of religious belief and tended to term the demonic, polluting, or irrational aspects as superstition, magic, taboo, or other "lower" forms of belief and behavior. In part this may have been due to his own religious persuasion, which considerably narrowed the scope of religious life to which he could respond with sensitivity and sympathy. Smith was able to view "lower" religions sociologically, but as a Christian he viewed

contemporary Christianity in absolute, intellectual terms. Thus, for him, early religions reflected a relative social reality, but Christianity was the product of revealed and true reality which transcended society and which was ultimately rooted in God and the individual. At times these biases led Smith to construct dichotomies involving society and the individual, magic and religion, pollution and purity, all of which impeded subsequent generations of writers on the sociology of religion.

Biblical Criticism and Theology

Since Smith wrote primarily for biblical and Semitic scholars, no study of his work, even one that is anthropological, can entirely neglect Smith's work and its relation to these fields. Unfortunately, the vastness and complexity of the literature involved make comment by any nonspecialist in these areas exceedingly risky. The best a commentator can do is to indicate what a few well-known and acknowledged experts report and to provide some references by which supplementary sources may be secured.

The sources of most of the interpretations which influenced Smith were the Continental biblical scholars of Germany and Holland, particularly the works of Julius Wellhausen and, to some extent, those of Abraham Kuenen. An accurate view of Smith's own evaluation of their work can be had through reading Smith's painstaking reviews, especially those in the *British and Foreign Evangelical Review,* Smith's introduction to the English translation of Wellhausen's work, and Smith's survey articles in the *Encyclopaedia Britannica,* especially "Bible" and "Hebrew Literature." Two modern studies may be helpful, both in their appraisal and review of biblical studies and their bibliographical material: Georg Fohrer, *Introduction to the Old Testament* (London: Society for Promoting Christian Knowledge, 1970), and Simon John DeVries, *Bible and Theology in the Netherlands* (Wageningen: H. Vrenman and Zonen, 1968), especially the section on Kuenen and his followers.

In his own day Smith complained about the parochiality of his theological colleagues who were ignorant of the important contemporary work done in German, Dutch, and French; one can well make the same complaints today where shoddy scholarship and ignorance of foreign sources characterize much of the writing in contemporary cultural anthropology.

The new biblical criticism which Smith embraced and which, in his day, was brilliantly epitomized by Julius Wellhausen and Abraham Kuenen, is generally conceded to have had its beginnings in the works of two Germans, Ferdinand C. Baur (1792–1860) and his follower, David F. Strauss (1808–74). Their approach, far more antireligious than that of many who followed, subjected sacred texts to the same methods of criticism which would be applied to any other body of writing. Besides applying their own commonsense and knowledge of what was plausible and possible (they did not countenance miraculous events or fantastic changes in character or in motivation), they emphasized the intensive analysis of material as it formed a particular whole in time and place. This second aspect of their work led to a form of historical and cultural relativism in the analysis by such writers as Kuenen, Wellhausen, and Smith. For example, a complex body of writing such as the Pentateuch was subjected to analyses of style, content, social references, and the like and demonstrated to have been written by several different authors over several periods of history. It may be remembered that it was views such as this that got Smith removed from his professorship at Aberdeen; today such an interpretation is generally held by most serious biblical scholars, regardless of their particular church affiliation. What this meant in terms of a historical or anthropological approach was this: the critic was required to master a very wide range of skills, from languages and etymology to archaeology, geography, comparative social studies, and the principles of technology. With these he might then evaluate and analyze such biblical texts, discerning their proper contextual meanings, detecting later changes or additions by careless or biased scribes, separating out what were once treated as integral sections into fragments written at different periods by different authors. These complex critical steps reflected two qualities essential to all good cultural anthropology and all good history: (1) the mastery of a culture as a totality, an appreciation of the wholeness of social phenomena; (2) the ability to try, as best one can, to view a culture from within, whether that be in terms of a different place and set of values (as the cultural anthropologist does) or in terms of different time, values, and perhaps place as well (as in the case of the historian and archaeologist). Thus, the qualities that made a good biblical scholar were, at least for Smith and those he admired, identical with those which would have made a good anthropologist or historian. Very early in his career, Smith wrote:

The fundamental principle of the higher criticism lies in the conception of the organic unity of all history. We must not see in history only a medley of petty dramas involving no higher springs of action than the passions and interests of individuals. History is not a stage-play, but the life and life-work of mankind continually unfolding in one great plan. And hence we have no true history where we cannot pierce through the outer shell of tradition into the life of a past age, mirrored in the living record of men who were themselves eyewitnesses and actors in the scenes they describe. Not mere facts, but the inner kernel of true life, is what the critical student delights to find in every genuine monument of antiquity; and the existence of such a kernel is to him the last criterion of historical authenticity. A tradition that violates the continuity of historical evolution and stands in no necessary relation to the conditions of the preceding and following age must be untrue; and, above all, an ancient writing is no frigid product of the school, but is instinct with true life, must be the product of that age which contained the conditions of the life it unconsciously reflects.[42]

It is of considerable significance that what is perhaps the first serious philosophical critique of history in modern English, Francis Herbert Bradley's *The Presuppositions of Critical History*,[43] was written in response to the critical approaches of Baur and Strauss, the German founders of the new criticism. Bradley's brilliant study emphasizes two essential issues: (1) "It is mere nonsense to talk of anything as 'an historical fact' unless criticism has been able to guarantee it as such." (2) "The facts which exist for critical history are events and recorded events. They are recorded, and that is to say that, although the work of the mind, they now at any rate are no mere feelings, nor generally the private contents of this or that man's consciousness, but are fixed and made outward, permanent, and accessible to the minds of all men."[44]

While still a student, Smith wrote:

History that merely balances probabilities is never certain; but where we have a historian in whose works we may so far read his character, we have a basis for higher certainty. In estimating the evidence of an event,

---

42. "The Question of Prophecy in the Critical Schools of the Continent" (1870), *LE*, pp. 164–65.

43. (Oxford: Parker, 1874); paper reprint, ed. Lionel Rubinoff (Chicago: Quadrangle, 1966).

44. Ibid. (1966 ed.), pp. 123, 89.

each man must learn for himself to enter into the historian's mind. The argument can never be reduced to mere calculation. And yet we do not find that the standard of historical truth is necessarily vague or doubt-ful, and therefore we must conclude that one man can really be known by others even if we have only his writings or actions before us, and never met him face to face.[45]

From Bradley's second point two problems follow, only one of which seems to have been fully appreciated by Smith. Smith, of course, grasped that the minds of men were indeed different in perspective and values at different periods. Indeed, his relation of ideas to the social behavior and social situation of a particular time and place was the strongest and most enduring of his analytical virtues. He repeatedly emphasized, as did Maine and Fustel de Coulanges writing of other peoples, that one could not present peoples such as the pre-exilic Hebrews or even the pagan Arabs as perceiving the world in terms such as our own or even in terms held at the time of Christ. However, Smith maintained that despite these differences, the sensitive critic could sympathetically project himself into these different periods. For Smith, all men, due to the nature of their reason, consciousness, imagination, and social experience, can with training and effort transcend, at least to some extent, the limitations in value and perception imposed by time, space, and culture. All this must be held if we are to have any history, anthropology, comparative sociology, or even comparative studies in literature, art, or music. The issue which he did not fully face and indeed which Bradley himself did not entirely dispose of involves the problem of the writer's own cultural milieu and its part in determining and limiting his perception. As Bradley himself notes, "in the field of history it is impossible to free ourselves from reasoning, and that in every case that which is called the fact is in reality a theory."[46] Smith's own social optimism regarding the high attainment of Victorian reason and his assumptions about a permanent and absolute set of Christian values may have prevented him from raising these issues. The question of the meaning of history and its relation to anthropology has been eloquently presented by R. B. Collingwood, *The Idea of History* (Ox-ford: Clarendon Press, 1946; London: Oxford University Press, 1961)

45. "Christianity and the Supernatural" (1869), *LE,* p. 112.

46. *Presuppositions,* p. 93.

and elsewhere dealt with by such writers as Michael Oakeshott, *Experience and Its Modes* (Cambridge: Cambridge University Press, 1933; new ed., 1966), pp. 90–168; and Peter Winch, *The Idea of a Social Science* (Cambridge: Cambridge Uniersity Press, 1958). Certainly Evans-Pritchard, himself an undergraduate in history at Oxford during the heyday of Collingwood,[47] has had this in mind with his insistence upon the similarity between anthropology and history. His observation that translation is the basic problem in social anthropology may be viewed as another way of stating this same phenomenological problem.[48]

Smith clearly owes many of his most striking theories to his predecessors in biblical criticism. His theory of sacrifice derives from Wellhausen, as do his emphasis upon the group rather than upon the individual in early religious beliefs and his interest in prophets as innovators. The most prominent of these influences will be cited as I deal with each of these issues. It is enough here to note that while it was Smith who framed these theories in striking and sociological form, he owed an immense debt to a biblical scholarly tradition which in many respects represented some of the most sophisticated social and historical analyses of the period.

Mother-Right and Totemism

The most obvious flaws in the *Lectures* relate to Smith's commitment to McLennan's theories of social evolution, totemism, and the use of survivals to reconstruct past phases of social life.[49] Others such as Spencer, Tylor, and Morgan had developed somewhat similar notions, but clearly McLennan's was the paramount anthropological influence

---

47.   Evans-Pritchard, however, indicates that his own full appreciation of Collingwood came only much later, after he had left Oxford as a student (personal communication).

48.   E. E. Evans-Pritchard, *Theories of Primitive Religion* (Oxford: Clarendon Press, 1965), pp. 10–14. In this same work Evans-Pritchard deals specifically with the relation between ideological bias and the analysis of religion. In taking some of his illustrious predecessors to task, he describes them as atheists and agnostics and therefore unsympathetic to religion (ibid., pp. 14–15); it is unfortunate that he omits Smith from this discussion for some of Smith's weaknesses in analysis and perception (as well as his strengths) derive from his particular religious convictions.

49.   John F. McLennan, *Primitive Marriage,* 1st ed. (Edinburgh: A. and C. Black, 1865; Chicago: University of Chicago, 1970); idem, "The Worship of Animals and Plants," *The Fortnightly Review* 6 (October 1869): 407–27; ibid. 6 (November 1869): 562–82; ibid. 7 (February 1870): 194–216.

on Smith.[50] Though such notions are mainly discredited today, they were then held by many social theorists, and Smith's work was praised by many of his contemporaries for the very reasons for which we now find the most serious faults.

Smith insisted that the early Semites were matrilineal and indeed were either ignorant of or unconcerned with the role of fathers in kinship. However, this theory has little to do with the main arguments of the *Lectures*. Smith does not emphasize these issues there since he felt that he had already successfully argued these points in his *Kinship and Marriage*. Indeed, other notable scholars, such as Goldziher and Wilken, had written further to support this position.[51] Even Frazer, who later rejected many of Smith's views on totemism, appears to have accepted most of them during Smith's lifetime. Smith himself, while crediting his views to McLennan, may well have been encouraged by other Semiticists; though he does not cite Baudissin favorably,[52] he was familiar with his work, which catalogs early Semitic religious beliefs according to the types of sanctuaries to which they are related; that is, those related to trees, to astral bodies, and to topographical objects of veneration.

It is worth noting that a large number of writers uncritically accepted Smith's views on totemism for many years after his death. Totemic theory was modified and expanded by Frazer into a useless hodgepodge

---

50.   Harris asserts that Smith's sociological interpretation of religion reflects the influence of Herbert Spencer; see Marvin Harris, *The Rise of Anthropological Theory* (New York: Crowell, 1968), p. 208. I can find little basis for this claim; biblical scholars and McLennan's writings provide ample inspiration for Smith's ideas. Smith read Spencer while a student at Edinburgh and found that "in Spencer's book the fallacies are very obvious" (*Life*, pp. 80-81). Smith met Spencer briefly in Cairo in the winter of 1879 and found him a very tedious person (ibid., p. 333).

51.   Ignácz Goldziher, "Le culte des ancêstres et le culte des morts chez les arabes," *Revue de l'histoire des religions* 10 (1884): 332-59; G. A. Wilken, *Das Matriarchat [Das Mutterrecht] beiden Alten Arabern* (Leipzig: Otto Schultze, 1884); Julius Wellhausen, *Reste Arabischen Heidentums* (Berlin: Reimer, 1897); Salomon Reinach, review of Hermann Strack, *Das Blut im Glauben und Aberglauben der Menschheit*, in *Revue des études juives* 41 (1900): 158; for useful citations of Continental literature supporting and criticizing Smith, see Wilhelm Schmidt, *The Origins and Growth of Religion* (New York: Dial, 1931), pp. 13-17; and M-F. Lagrange, *Etudes des religions sémitiques* (Paris: Librairie V. Lecoffre, 1903), pp. 112-13, 244-68.

52.   Wolf Wilhelm, Grafen Baudissin, *Studien zur semitischen Religionsgeschichte* (Leipzig: Fr. Wilh. Grunow, 1876-78). Smith ignores Baudissin in the *LRS* but attacks him in "Animal Tribes" (1880).

of descriptive material and was justly criticized by scholars such as Goldenweiser. Nonetheless, nonanthropologists such as Cook, Jevons, Harrison, Freud, and Reik,[53] through their influential texts on the history and origins of religions, kept Smith's notions current in philosophical, psychological, and biblical studies, even though these were often in forms highly distorted and naive, due to Frazerian influence. This is not to suggest that all Semitic scholars accepted such views. Thus the great French Semiticist, Fr. Lagrange writes of Smith's work: "il est constamment dominé par une idée fausse, l'importance exagerée du totémisme dans l'histoire de la religion. Comme il arrive ordinairement, les éleves ont été encore plus systématiques que le maitre, d'où l'inondation de totémisme dont nous avons souffert."[54]

Undisputably, Smith was a major figure in creating a popular interest in totemism. Freud and Durkheim accepted Smith's data uncritically, even though Smith's scholarly evidence for early Semitic mother-right and totemism is very questionable and discredited today.[55] His was a kind of reconstruction based on the worst forms of conjectural history founded on the doctrine of survivals.[56] Certainly his insistence that early

53. Stanley A. Cook, *The Foundations of Religion* (London: T. C. and E. C. Jack, n.d.), esp. pp. 77-78; Frank Byron Jevons, *An Introduction to the History of Religion* (1st ed. 1896); 5th ed., London: Methuen, 1911), pp. v, 12-13, 96-107; Jane E. Harrison, *Themis* (1912; reprint ed., New York: World, 1962), accepts Smith's notions on the nonindividuality of ancient religions and his communal theory of sacrifice, but significantly rejects his valuable notion of subordinating myth to ritual (pp. 28-29, 136, 329). Sigmund Freud, *Totem und Tabu* (1913); English trans., "Totem and Taboo," in *Basic Writings of Sigmund Freud*, ed. A. A. Brill (New York: Random House, 1938), pp. 909-26; Theodor Reik, *Ritual: Psycho-Analytic Studies* (1931; reprint ed., New York: Farrar, Strauss, 1946), pp. 17-19, 188, 299. Wundt never cites Smith, but maintains that animal worship is a necessary first stage in the evolution of religious beliefs and practices; see W. Wundt, *Völkerpsychologie* (1906; reprint ed., Leipzig: A. Kröner, 1922), 2, pt. 2: 236.

54. *Etudes*, p. ix; see also ibid., pp. 112-13, where Lagrange cites other Continental Semiticists who attacked Smith's views. See also Alfred Loisy, *Essai historique sur le sacrifice* (Paris: E. Nourry, 1920), pp. 5-6.

55. For three very useful historical surveys of views on totemism and its relation to Smith's theories of sacrifice, all rejecting Smith's views, see A. van Gennep, *L'état actuel du problème totémique* (Paris: E. Leroux, 1920), esp. pp. 17, 53, 94, 105, 143, 145, 180, 192, 234-35, 250, 282, 308, 311, 330, 341; Edgar Reuterskioeld, "Der Totemismus," in *Archiv für Religionswissenschaft nach Albrecht Dieterich*, ed. Richard Wünsch, 15 (Leipzig: B. G. Teubner, 1912): 1-23. Certainly the most comprehensive survey of reactions to Smith's theories in his own time is Stanley A. Cook, "Israel and Totemism," *The Jewish Quarterly Review* 14 (August 1902): 413-48. For sources on more recent research in ancient Arab institutions, see Joseph Chelhod, *Le sacrifice chez les arabes, recherches sur l'évolution, la nature et la fonction des rites sacrificiels en Arabie*

man was totemic in religion and never polytheistic, much less monotheistic, is now generally rejected. Smith presents his own theory of sacrifice as essentially related to totemism, and he relates what he considers
the primordial form of sacrifice to communal and commensal rites
deriving from a sacrificial devouring of a totem by those who venerate
it. In later pages I consider some of the difficulties in this theory as well
as some of the alternatives.

Evolutionism, Society, and the Individual

Smith's evolution is a curious combination of Victorian anthropological
notions of progress and Christian notions about the gradual enlightenment and moral perfectability of man. Thus, primitive man is described
as less critical, less rational, more fear-ridden, and less inclined to
introspective, individualistic thought than modern man, who is described as less dominated by habit or custom but consciously and ration-
ally reaching theological and moral conceptions superior to his predecessors. Evolution makes sense if one believes, as Smith did, in a chosen
people for whom truths were slowly revealed over a long period of
history. Thus, Smith saw Jews as gradually evolving from a period of
ignorance about God's plans for them through ever higher forms of
moral awareness, with Christian revelation representing the evolutionary peak. The prophets provided the key force in this progress. The new
biblical criticism further demonstrated that some progress was still
possible in the sense that although Christ had spoken the final truth, his
message had been recorded by human scribes and the distortions and
omissions due to time and human error had still to be corrected through
scholarly research.

Smith's evolutionary approach further required that he account for
the persistance of "lower," less rational forms of thought and behavior,

---

occidentale (Paris: Presses universitaires de France, 1955), esp. pp. 181-83. The value of
Chelhod's work is contested by some Semiticists, but he does have the virtue of some
sociological orientation; see Maxime Rodinson, review of Chelhod, Le sacrifice, in Revue
de l'histoire des religions 150 (1956): 232-41. For a more conservative and cautious set of
statements with little interpretation, see G. Ryckmans, Les religions arabes préislamiques,
Revue d'études orientales, no. 26 (Louvain: Le Muséum, 1951).

56.   For an excellent discussion of the part this notion played in Victorian anthropology,
see Margaret T. Hodgen, The Doctrine of Survivals (London: Alleson, 1936). Hodgen
clearly notes that while Smith also distorted material through his use of this concept, he
still was able to assume a more constructive position in opposition to Tylor, perhaps the
most baneful influence in regard to these ideas (pp. 111-12).

even after "higher" forms were exhibited by a people. He tried to do this through the use of the doctrine of survivals. This also, in a circular form of argument, allowed him to reconstruct the past. Any elements inconvenient to his theories could be excluded from a contemporary system by being identified as mere residue from the past, yet these same elements could still be utilized to describe and prove the nature of a preceding period.

Smith's evolutionary theories were complexly connected with those aspects of his thought which are most praised by present-day anthropologists. His emphasis upon the group setting of ritual was associated with his characterization of primitive religious behavior. For Smith, primitive peoples were nonindividualistic in their religious consciousness. For him, group-held, communal values epitomized primitive life and thought. He characterized kinship and other jural demands as jointly held by all within a lineage or kindred, and he reasoned that this indicated that the beliefs behind these groupings were also held uniformly. This is odd, because elsewhere he observed that what really mattered was not what such people thought, but how they behaved, implying that there could be a considerable variation in the beliefs held by such people.

Given this view of the earliest forms of social and religious thought, Smith had to account for the changes which led to the present stage of religious life. And because of his Christian and Victorian beliefs, he tended to view such change in terms of a progression toward higher and truer forms of belief and ethical behavior. Not only was Christianity an improvement on Judaism, but, for Smith, Presbyterianism was a higher form of Christianity than Roman Catholicism; and even among Presbyterians, Smith felt that study and examination of the Bible would create an ever improved breed.

Smith seems to have made few if any comments on any complex religious systems other than those derived from Semitic culture. Despite the great advances in the studies of the religions of the Far East which had occurred during the Victorian period, Hinduism, Buddhism, and other such cosmological systems have no part in his developmental theories. Even in terms of Semitic studies, his work is sadly deficient in a proper appreciation of what was then understood about neighboring Egyptian and Assyrian civilizations. While Smith clearly believed in certain rational and moral qualities being potential in the minds of all, for him it required the heroic and imaginative innovations of Judeo-

Christian prophets to lead men upward toward a higher consciousness of God's essence and will and toward a more ethical and civilized mode of social interaction. This, of course, is a view of social change consistent with Christian theology, with its concentration on the innovative prophet from Moses to Christ. It mattered little that these prophets presented their new views merely as clearer, more accurate formulations of a basic truth that had to be seen as changeless from the beginning.

Because of his views on social change and religious innovation, Smith was led to associate the higher forms of religious life with the individual rather than with the social group. The social group was epitomized by custom and socially sanctioned ritual and was led by a priest, often in the service of a king. The innovative, individual prophet, while speaking in terms of social values and morality, ultimately stood outside the temporary and relative frame of reference of the present social status quo; the conservative social group was contrasted with the innovative individual conscience, the priest-king with the prophet. This is a side of Smith's thought often ignored today when Smith is chiefly remembered as Durkheim's precursor in a theory of the social basis of religious behavior.

It should thus be obvious that Smith's views of both the group and the individual were very ambiguous. A prophet, while innovative or reformist, could only speak to his own time. A prophet could only convey his message in terms meaningful to his own society. Thus, while all of God's prophets presented some form of the truth, men were, as their awareness improved, prepared for ever more complex and higher forms of prophetic revelation. This interpretation allowed Smith to develop a highly sophisticated cultural-historical methodology, and it also allowed him to resolve any conflict that might be raised between the belief in God's invariable truth and the manifestly different moral and theological perspectives evinced over the centuries of biblical chronicles. Thus, while God's ultimate message was ever the same, men and society in which men lived and from which much of men's perspectives derived were manifested in different forms and levels of development in history. A prophet could only present God's word in terms meaningful within that time and culture. Prophets could therefore innovate, but never so far as to be incredible and meaningless to the people and modes of thought of a particular time. Prophets could be "ahead" of their society and time, but never too far. They were the convenient diachronic link between different synchronic stages of society. The elements of Smith's theological analysis (and those of many other biblical scholars) closely parallel the ideas of Marx and others concerned with social change and social awareness. Individual invention, the self-interest of individuals or particular groups, the alienation of intellectuals or certain classes, the moral awareness of profoundly spiritual individual men — all these serve as useful analytical devices whereby theorists may portray dysfunction, conflict, and change in a system elsewhere described as cohesive and stable.

Evolutionism and the Historical-Functionalist Method

Another aspect of Smith's approach led to the refinement of his analytical techniques for understanding a particular stage of culture and society. Thus, to grasp the message of Ezekiel, one must first reconstruct not only the social organization of that prophet's time but also its cosmology and mode of thought and expression. If Ezekiel's message is clearly different in some respects from that of Samuel, this is not because of any contradiction in the overriding messages of the Bible; rather, it is simply due to the fact that the society, problems, and modes of thought during Samuel's time were vastly different from those during the Exile. Smith and every reputable biblical scholar of his day and after develop an interpretation of a scriptural passage within terms of the language, society, and cosmology of the time contemporary with it. An anthropologist, a historian, an art or literary critic must perforce do the same.

Smith's views of the individual and society, however, are more complex than a mere portrayal of the individual as the positive innovator against and "above" static society. Smith also viewed the individual in a negative manner. For him, magic and many other aspects of social behavior are not particularly social (and therefore ethical) but rather are manifestations of individual thought and activity as it operates outside and "beneath" society. The individual is not thoroughly integrated into the social aspects of human life, and therefore he continues to rely on simpler, more primitive aspects of behavior and thought. These views were held because Smith could not fit demonic or polluting aspects of belief and behavior into a model of a cosmology and society of which he approved. When these occurred in Judaic or Christian thought, they were expunged from the social and relegated to being the survivals in individuals of earlier, more primitive beliefs and behavior. Smith constructed this model of a dichotomy between the individual and society in order to deal with his revulsion toward those aspects of his data which offended his sense of the moral, spiritual, and rational; ironically, another moralistic writer, Freud, adapted these views to his theory of the subconscious.

Smith resembles Durkheim in visualizing the individual as the battleground between society and nature. The innovative individual, as epitomized by the prophet, represents the moral culmination of society, an expression of its best qualities leading society toward a clearer realization of its highest values. And like Durkheim, Smith saw the greatest men of this sort as deeply altruistic. In sharp contrast to his conception of the prophet, Smith visualized some individuals as holding ideas and behaving in ways not only outside society but contradictory to its very welfare. The practitioners of magic are prime examples of such retrograde individuals. The idea of the deviant remains central to the works of both Smith and Durkheim; he is valued positively or negatively depending upon the values and definitions of a particular society. Both Smith and Durkheim posit these values as relative to the state of society at a particular time, but in practice both tend to derive their evaluations from their own moralistic assumptions and needs; each betrays his own deepest values about what society should and must be.

The Changing Evaluation of Smith's Achievement

We have seen that many of Smith's distinguished colleagues, such as Wilken, Goldziher, and Wellhausen, admired his work. They and their followers perpetuated many of Smith's anthropological notions. As a result one finds that many, though far from all, in the fields of biblical and Semitic studies utilized a set of anthropological theories about totemism, mother-right, and sacrifice long after these had been abandoned by most in anthropology itself.[57] This led Snaith, in a

---

57. See earlier discussion and footnotes for references to Wilken, Goldziher, and Wellhausen; see also Jevons, *Introduction,* esp. pp. 12-13, 96-118; Cook, *Foundations;* W. O. E. Oesterley and T. H. Robinson, *Hebrew Religion: Its Origin and Development* (London: Society for Promoting Christian Knowledge, 1930), esp. pp. 4-17; W. O. E. Oesterley, *Sacrifices in Ancient Israel: Their Origins, Purposes and Development* (London: Hodder and Stoughton, 1937), pp. 154-71; R. A. S. Macalister,

highly respected survey of biblical studies, to lament that while it was surely all to the good that biblical scholars had studied the religions of primitive and exotic peoples, what had begun as a useful supplementary perspective had become a preoccupation which seriously distorted the nature of the material.[58]

Furthermore, it was also highly questionable whether Smith had much justification in assuming that the Arab Bedouin exhibited a way of life essentially like that of the Semitic forebears of the ancient Jews. Today Smith's stereotype of the purely nomadic Ur-Semite as the precursor of Judaism or even Islam is increasingly rejected by most as oversimplification: "Any study of the Old Testament institutions must begin with an investigation into nomadism. . . . Even in the comparatively small area of the Middle East, there have always been different types of nomads, and what is true of one type is not necessarily true of another. . . . Once he begins to raise cattle as well as flocks, the shepherd ceases to be a true nomad. Neither the Israelites nor their ancestors were ever true Bedouin, that is, camel-breeders. Their fathers kept sheep and goats, and when we first meet them in history, the Patriarchs are already becoming a settled people. This is one factor which puts limits on the comparisons which can be drawn from the Bedouin whom ethnographers have studied."[59]

"Sacrifice (Semitic)," *Encyclopaedia of Religion and Ethics*, ed. James Hastings (New York: Scribners, 1951), pp. 31–38. For a brief and hostile summary and reference list of works responding to Smith's totemic theories, see Wilhelm Schmidt, *Origins*, pp. 103–17.

58.   Norman H. Snaith, *The Distinctive Ideas of the Old Testament* (London: Epworth, 1944), esp. pp. 11–13. Significantly, Franz Steiner frequently cites Snaith in his critique of Smith; see *Taboo* (London: Cohen and West, 1956), pp. 78–86.

59.   Roland de Vaux, O.P., *Ancient Israel: Its Life and Institutions*, 2 vols. [*Les institutions de l'ancien Testament*, 1958, 1960] (New York: McGraw-Hill, 1965), 1: 3–4. De Vaux presents an excellent summary and useful set of references for these issues (pp. 3–14). Fr. Lagrange wrote with perception of how Smith makes questionable use of exotic materials from primitive societies yet ignores the rich cuneiform material from Babylonia. He explains this as partly due to Smith's dubious assumption that contemporary Bedouin society provides a model of ancient Semitic culture and that primitive peoples are everywhere similar, and partly due to his own refusal to consider written sources as reflecting ancient modes of thought as authentically as oral tradition (p.66). While Smith's use of comparative data from exotic societies is sometimes incautious, such abuses never reach the degrees of those of Frazer, Cook, or Jevons. In any case, Smith's emphasis on the Bedouin roots of some aspects of Hebrew sacrifice and his stress upon western Semitic rather than Babylonian material may have been right after all; see Roland de Vaux, O.P., *Studies in Old Testament Sacrifice* (Cardiff: University of Wales, 1964), pp. 15–20.

Table 1

Principal Works of the Period with Special Relevance to Smith's Work

1861–65	A. Kuenen. *Historisch-kritisch Onderzoek naar het verzameling van de boeken des Ouden Verbands.* Haarlem.
1864	N. Fustel de Coulanges. *Le cité antique.* Paris.
1865	E. B. Tylor. *Researches into the Early History of Mankind.* London.
1865	J. F. McLennan. *Primitive Marriage.* Edinburgh.
1869–79	J. F. McLennan. "The Worship of Animals and Plants." London.
1869–70	A. Kuenen. *De Godsdienst van Israel.* Haarlem.
1871–73	E. Ewald. *Die Lehre der Bibel von Gott.* Leipzig.
1871	E. B. Tylor. *Primitive Culture.* London.
1871	E. B. Bradley. *The Presuppositions of Critical History.* Oxford.
1876–77	J. Wellhausen. *Die Composition des Hexateuchs und der historischen Bücher des Alten Testament.* Berlin.
1876	J. F. McLennan. *Studies in Ancient History.* London.
1876–78	Graf Baudissin. *Studien zur semitischen Religionsgeschichte.* Leipzig.
1878	J. Wellhausen. *Prolegomena zur Geschichte Israels.* Berlin.
1878	F. M. Müller. *Lectures on the Origin and Growth of Religion.* London.
1885	W. R. Smith. *Kinship and Marriage in Early Arabia.* Cambridge.

1885-88	F. Ratzel.
	Völkerkunde. Leipzig.
1887	E. Renan.
	Histoire du peuple d'Israël. Paris.
1887	J. G. Frazer.
	Totemism. Edinburgh.
1889	W. R. Smith.
	Lectures on the Religion of the Semites. Edinburgh.
1890	J. G. Frazer.
	The Golden Bough. London.
1893	E. Durkheim.
	De la division du travail social. Paris.
1896	F. B. Jevons.
	An Introduction to the History of Religion. London.
1898	H. Hubert and M. Mauss.
	"Essai sur la nature et la fonction du sacrifice." Paris.
1898	S. Lévi.
	"La doctrine du sacrifice dans les Brâhmanas." Paris.
1899	E. Durkheim.
	"De la définition des phénoménes religieux." Paris.
1900-09	W. Wundt.
	Völkerpsychologie. Leipzig.
1903	E. Durkheim and M. Mauss.
	"De quelques formes primitives classification." Paris.
1904	H. Hubert and M. Mauss.
	"Esquisse d'une théorie générale de la magie." Paris.
1909	A. van Gennep.
	Les rites de passage. Paris.
1909	R. R. Marett.
	The Threshold of Religion. London.
1910	L. Lévy-Bruhl.
	Les fonctions mentales dans les sociétés inférieures. Paris.
1912	E. Durkheim.
	Les formes élémentaires de la vie religieuses. Paris.
1913	S. Freud.
	"Totem und Tabu." Vienna.

Of course, some criticism was leveled against Smith from the first, and not all of this was from the conservative interpreters of the Bible. In his review of Smith's book, the famous Assyriologist Sayce wrote:

I must enter a protest against the assumption that what holds good of Kaffirs or Australians held good also for the primitive Semite. The students of language have at last learnt that what is applicable to one family of speech is not necessarily applicable to another, and it would be well if the anthropologist would learn the same lesson. Prof. Robertson Smith, for instance, assumes that Semitic society began with a matriarchate, since it has been shown that in a large number of early communities the family was represented by the mother. But for such an assumption I can see no evidence.[60]

Sayce's views are not so different from present-day criticism of abuse of the comparative method in biblical studies:

Historians of comparative religion are tempted to misuse the comparative method, and to bring forward, as an explanation of Israelite sacrifice, the practices or the ideas of peoples with different religious concepts; in particular, they look for analogies between Israelite ritual and the customs of so-called "primitive" peoples, for among these primitive peoples, they claim, we find the fundamental significance of ritual. Theologians, on the other hand, tend to use the sacrifice of the New Testament (and subsequent Christian doctrinal interpretations of it) in order to explain the true meaning of Old Testament sacrifice. Both parties tend to neglect or to underrate elements which may be proper to Israelite sacrifice.[61]

Sayce went on to publish general attacks against much of the new criticism for ignoring archaeological evidence, for assuming a much later date for the advent of writing than was warranted and thereby refusing to assign certain material to its proper early date, for having underestimated or distorted the relations between the culture of Israel and those of Egypt and Assyria, for giving too much emphasis to details of philology and literary style in interpreting the social meaning

---

60.   A. H. Sayce, review of *LRS*, in *The Academy* 36 (30 November 1889): 357-58. Smith wrote a peevish rejoinder in the next issue. Contrast this review with an anonymous laudatory but conservative one in *Nature* (13 February 1890), pp. 337-38.

61.   de Vaux, *Ancient Israel*, p. 447.

and dates of texts, and for using the comparative method in a careless manner which led to unjustified assumptions and generalizations.[62]

Undoubtedly the most important criticisms in Smith's own view were those of the German biblical scholars. Karl Budde wrote a long and careful review praising the book's breadth of scholarship and the originality of its insights but criticizing many of Smith's conclusions as mere conjecture and as being highly problematic. He also justly pointed out Smith's oversimplification of the heterogeneous sources of Semitic thought, and his tendency toward underplaying those aspects which some might consider peculiar to that cultural tradition. As Budde rightly observed, Smith had entitled his book a study of Semitic religion, but what he had sought was the very source of all religion. His data were not commensurate with his aims. Budde appreciated the grandeur of Smith's questions, but he was rightly disturbed by Smith's incautious treatment of the details in order to make his points. Budde generously concluded by hoping that at least some of these issues might be clarified in the proposed sequels that Smith, as it turned out, was prevented from completing due to ill health.[63]

Finally, it is ironic that within a decade after Smith's death, while biblical, Semitic, and even classical scholars continued to cite his work, in British anthropology his reputation had in large part been superceded by that of his protegé, James Frazer. Though Frazer himself dedicated *The Golden Bough* to Smith and considered Smith the greatest man he had ever known, his own work scarcely reflects the better and most enduring aspects of his mentor's views.[64] Both Andrew Lang and R. R. Marett briefly mention Smith, mainly as a source of information, but their theoretical discussions are directed almost

---

62. See A. H. Sayce, *The Early History of the Hebrews* (London: Rivingtons, 1899); and idem, *The "Higher Criticism" and the Verdict of the Monuments*, 2d ed. (London: Society for Promoting Christian Knowledge, 1894). Oddly, Sayce never mentions Smith by name in these criticisms, though he criticized Smith during the latter's lifetime.

63. Karl Budde, review of *LRS*, in *Theologische Literaturzeitung* 15, no. 22 (1 November 1890): 538-43.

64. R. A. Downie, *James George Frazer* (London: Watts, 1940), p. 9. J. W. Burrows aptly notes that although Frazer considered himself Smith's disciple, "Frazer wrote anthropology like Tylor, not like Robertson Smith" (*Evolution and Society* [Cambridge: Cambridge University Press, 1966], p. 241n).

entirely toward Frazer.[65] Hartland utilizes Smith's theories on totemism, mother-right, and blood covenant in a manner neither critical nor cautious.[66] Westermarck rejects Smith's theories on totemism and sacrifice and devotes far more attention to the views of Frazer.[67] In his well-known survey, Penniman goes so far as to refer to Smith as one who followed the views of Frazer,[68] while neither Lowie nor Nadel mention Smith at all in their surveys of the history of the discipline.[69] Curiously, despite Durkheim's deep admiration for Smith's work, his followers Hubert and Mauss, while critically examining Smith's views on sacrifice, ignore his work altogether in their scholarly treatise on magic. This is especially odd since these authors utilize the individual in a Smith-like manner in order to explain the secularization of magic.[70] In his pioneer study of totemism, van Gennep briefly refers to Smith's work and notes that his own findings are at odds with Smith's interpretation.[71]

Radcliffe-Brown, quoting extensively from the *Lectures,* warmly praises Smith for his views on the primacy of rites over belief.[72] However, it is Malinowski who in that generation seems the keenest

65.   Andrew Lang, *Magic and Religion* (London: Longmans, Green, 1901); idem, *Myth, Ritual and Religion* (London: Longmans, Green, 1887); R. R. Marett, *The Threshold of Religion* (London: Methuen, 1909).

66.   Edwin Sidney Hartland, *The Legend of Perseus,* 3 vols. (London: David Nutt, 1894-96), 2: 234-42.

67.   Edvard Westermarck, *The Origins and Development of the Moral Ideas,* 2d ed., 2 vols. (London: Macmillan, 1924-26), 2: 603-4, 623. E. O. James, an anthropologically oriented scholar of religion, pays little attention to Smith's theories, as contrasted to Frazer's; see his *Origins of Sacrifice* (1933; reprint ed., Port Washington, N. Y.: Kennikat, 1971).

68.   T. K. Penniman, *A Hundred Years of Anthropology,* reprint of 3d ed. (New York: International Universities Press, 1970), p. 143.

69.   Robert Lowie, *History of Ethnological Theory* (New York: Holt, Rinehart, and Winston, 1937); S. R. Nadel, *The Foundations of Social Anthropology* (Glencoe, Ill.; Free Press, 1951).

70.   Henri Hubert and Marcel Mauss, "Essai sur la nature et la fonction du sacrifice," *L'Année sociologique* (1898) — trans. W. D. Halls, *Sacrifice* (London: Cohen and West, 1964); idem, "Esquisse d'une théorie générale de la magie," *L'Année sociologique* (1902-03) — trans. R. Brain, *A General Theory of Magic* (London: Routledge, Kegan Paul, 1972).

71.   Arnold van Gennep, *Tabou et totémisme à Madagascar* (Paris: Bibliothèque de l'école des hautes études, sciences religieuses 17, 1904), pp. 143-44.

72.   A. R. Radcliffe-Brown, *Structure and Function in Primitive Society* (Glencoe, Ill: Free Press, 1952), pp. 155-56.

admirer of Smith:

As in many other matters we owe the first flash of insight to that great Scot scholar Robertson Smith. Robertson Smith was perhaps the first clearly to recognise the sociological aspect in all human religions and also to emphasise, at times perhaps to over-emphasise, the importance of ritual as against dogma. . . . In this, Robertson Smith recognises clearly that any narrative has to be assessed by the function that it plays in organised religious behaviour.[73]

More recently Smith has again been considered a serious source of analytical and theoretical insight, especially in the works of Franz Steiner, E. E. Evans-Pritchard, E. R. Leach, and Mary Douglas. Victor Turner's valuable writings on ritual often seem akin to Smith's, though Turner never mentions Smith's work. These authors in turn clearly derive much of their interest indirectly, through the influence which Smith's work exerted upon Durkheim, Hubert, and Mauss, Freud and Radcliffe-Brown. Clearly, in recent years there has been a renewed appreciation of the problems involved in the study of ritual, and in particular to its relation to beliefs and to the social groups in which these are held and practiced.

The Comparative Method

Frazer describes Smith as one of the founders of the comparative method in the study of religion.[74] Certainly he was among the very first to use such an approach anthropologically in biblical scholarship. His work exhibits most of the basic strengths and weaknesses of the comparative method. The use of such a method is only possible if one accepts the psychic unity of man and credits all societies as being subject to similar principles of development. Thus, Smith observes: "This

---

73. B. Malinowski, *Sex, Culture, and Myth* (New York: Harcourt, Brace, and World, 1962), p. 254.

74. *The Gorgon's Head*, p. 281. Frazer goes on to maintain that such studies inevitably lead to a reappraisal of a great proportion of religious beliefs and practices as "false and foolish," a view which hardly would have pleased his former teacher (ibid., p. 284). Hubert and Mauss castigate both Smith and Frazer in their use of the comparative method: "Robertson Smith's error was above all one of method. Instead of analysing in its original complexity the Semitic ritual system, he set about classifying the facts genealogically, in accordance with the analogical connexions that he believed he saw between them. This is a characteristic common to English [*sic*] anthropologists, who are concerned above all with collecting and classifying documents" *Sacrifice*, p. 7.

account of the position of religion in the social system holds good, I
believe, for all parts and races of the ancient world in the earlier stages
of their history. The causes of so remarkable a uniformity lie hidden in
the midst of prehistoric time, but must plainly have been of a general
kind, operating on all parts of mankind without distinction of race and
local environment; for in every region of the world, as soon as we find a
nation or tribe emerging from prehistoric darkness into the light of
authentic history, we find also that its religion conforms to the general
type which has just been indicated."[75] "But a careful study and
comparison of the various sources is sufficient to furnish a tolerably
accurate view of a series of general features which recur with striking
uniformity in all parts of the Semitic field, and govern the evolution of
faith and worship down to a late date."[76]

Smith's comparative method, like Durkheim's, proceeded along two
broader, interrelated theoretical lines, evolutionism and essentialism.
As an evolutionist, Smith sought to reconstruct the process and forms of
development which beliefs, social action, and social groupings took
through time:

The record of the religious thought of mankind, as it is embodied in
religious institutions, resembles the geological record of the history of
the earth's crust; the new and the old are preserved side by side, or
rather layer upon layer. The classification of ritual formations in their
proper sequence is the first step towards their explanation, and that
explanation itself must take the form, not of a speculative theory, but of
a rational life-history.[77]

The very possibility of reconstructing the history of human progress rests
on the fact that all over the world mankind has been moving in the same
general direction, but at very various rates, and that careful reasoning,
aided by the observations of cases which exhibit a state of transition
(e.g., from one type of kinship to another), enables us to bring out the
order in which the various observed types of social structure succeed one
another.[78]

75. *LRS*, p. 30.
76. Ibid., p. 15.
77. Ibid., p. 24.
78. Review of Edvard Westermarck's *The History of Human Marriage,* in *Nature* 44
(1891): 271.

Because more "advanced" societies had necessarily developed along generally similar lines, Smith maintained that earlier forms could be reconstructed by comparative study. This he often did through an ingenious but unacceptable employment of the concept of survivals. First, he maintained that elements from earlier stages tended to persist in distorted form long after they were no longer fully comprehended and were no longer an essential part of a social system. Once apprehended, these imperfect or fragmentary traits could then be fleshed out and more clearly perceived by the analyst through the study of other cultures presumably existing on a developmental level now surpassed by the society he had originally considered. Even in his lifetime Smith was sharply criticized for such methods. Sayce accused Smith of obtaining his interpretations from the ethnographic data of the primitive societies of many continents and then applying these findings to the sketchier data of the ancient Semitic world.[79] In reply Smith insisted, "I was led from the Semites to a wider generalization, and not conversely." Yet he himself gives away how arbitrary he was in evaluating the evidence when he asserts that "in religion, as in philology, the comparative method supplied the means of distinguishing between what is primitive and what is degenerate."[80] Making such judgments is as tricky as Durkheim's famous attempt to discern what is normal and what is abnormal by means of the comparative method.

But despite his belief in uniformities which justified comparative research, Smith's religious bias led him to separate Judaism, Islam, and Christianity ("positive religions") from the other, traditional, "unconscious" religious traditions which preceded them. He admitted that these were rooted in the past, yet he insisted that the dawning moral consciousness of a series of religious innovators drew the monotheistic religions out of the commoner level of group-oriented morality.[81]

Smith was also an essentialist; by that I mean that he sought to use the comparative method to isolate that which was most essential, most basic, to a social institution: "But the right point of departure for a general study of Semitic religion must be sought in regions where, though our knowledge begins at a later date, it refers to a simpler state

79. Sayce, The "Higher Criticism." See also Lagrange, Etudes, p. 66.
80. Letter, The Academy 36 (7 December 1889): 375.
81. LRS, pp. 1–2.

of society, and where accordingly the religious phenomena revealed to us are of an origin less doubtful and a character less complicated."[82]

In a phrase strikingly close to Durkheim, Smith states that "spiritual and moral principles, like material organisms, are more easily understood in their germinal form."[83] Pursuing this mode of thought Smith concluded that sacrifice was the central and most basic rite of all religions:

The problem does not belong to any one religion, for sacrifice is equally important among all early peoples in all parts of the world where religious ritual has reached any considerable development. Here, therefore, we have to deal with an institution that must have been shaped by the action of general causes, operating very widely and under conditions that were common in primitive times to all races of mankind. To construct a theory of sacrifice exclusively on the Semitic evidence would be unscientific and misleading, but for the present purpose it is right to put the facts attested for the Semitic peoples in the foreground, and to call in the sacrifices of other nations to confirm or modify the conclusions to which we are led.[84]

While Smith sought essentials by sifting out the common elements which endured through each evolutionary phase of development, his examination of data was focused upon one culture area. Again, like Durkheim who followed him, Smith seemed to feel that a few cases strategically chosen could serve to elucidate matters for a far wider set of situations.[85] Since Smith regarded Christianity as holding the ultimate fulfillment in religious consciousness and activities, so the examination of its roots and development should contain in refined terms, all (though also more) that is and was held in other religions as well.

82.   Ibid., p. 14.

83.   "The Attitude of Christians to the Old Testament," *Expositor,* 2d ser., 7 (1884): 251.

84.   *LRS,* p. 214; this was Smith's position even earlier in his famous essay, "Sacrifice," *EB* 21 (1886): 135.

85.   The validity of Smith's assumption of a common Semitic tradition is a complex issue, and certainly Smith does seem to have underemphasized the outside influences upon the area. Smith's preoccupation with pastoral nomadism reflects this, for he reasoned that since the ancient Hebrews were pastoral, they were not easily accessible to outside influences, not even during their stay in Egypt (*The Prophets of Israel,* 1919 ed., pp. 379-80; see entry in Bibliography).

Sacrifice

Over half of the *Lectures* are devoted to the topic of sacrifice, and it is unquestionably Smith's views on this that have attracted most discussion.[86] While few today would support his analysis of sacrifice, probably still fewer would disagree with him that "the origin and meaning of sacrifice constitute the central problem of ancient religion."[87] In part this is a result of Smith's emphasis upon ritual and group fellowship over belief and theology. More important, this springs from the primary importance of Christ's sacrifice in all Christian thought: "Thus, when we wish thoroughly to study the New Testament doctrine of sacrifice, we are carried back step by step till we reach a point where we have to ask what sacrifice meant, not only to the old Hebrews alone, but to the whole circle of nations of which they formed a part."[88]

Smith wrote at a period when the gift theory of sacrifice as developed by Tylor prevailed in anthropological circles.[89] Smith rejected this as a less basic function.[90] Instead, he maintained that the most basic sacrifice from which all other forms derived involved an act of communion between a social group and a supernatural being with which that group sought to reaffirm its union. The most primordial form of this was a religious feast at which the group killed and ate the totemic animal from which they thought themselves descended. Smith went on to postulate that with domestication of animals, the veneration of nurtured livestock led to their replacing the wild totemic animal in later sacrifices. He then contrasted sacrifice of domestic produce,

86.   Besides the general works by de Vaux, Oesterley, Chelhod, Loisy, Lagrange, Snaith, and Hubert and Mauss already cited, the reader might consult Georges Gusdorf, *L'éxperience humain du sacrifice* (Paris: Presses universitaires de France, 1948), although I did not find this particularly helpful. The most useful recent survey devoted to reevaluating Smith's views is R. J. Thompson, *Penitence and Sacrifice in Early Israel outside the Levitical Law* (Leiden: E. J. Brill, 1963). However, de Vaux, *Studies,* is perhaps the single most useful general survey of these issues.

87.   *LRS,* p. 27; Smith's point is essentially the same as Loisy, *Essai,* p. 1; see also E. E. Evans-Pritchard, Introduction to Hubert and Mauss, *Sacrifice,* pp. vii-viii; and E. Durkheim, *The Elementary Forms of the Religious Life (Les formes élémentaires de la vie religieuse,* 1912), trans. J. W. Swain (London: Allen and Unwin, 1912), p. 336.

88.   *LRS,* p. 3.

89.   Sir Edward B. Tylor, *Primitive Culture,* pt. 2 (1871; paperback ed., New York: Harper, 1958), pp. 461-62.

90.   *LRS,* p. 393.

positing nomadic pastoralism as invariably preceding sedentary agriculture, and therefore communion sacrifice preceding tributary.[91] Smith rejected not only the gift theory but with it the notions of tribute, expiation, guilt, and solemnity. All these aspects of sacrifice were said by him to postdate the joyful, totemic feast of communion. The latter was presented as an expression of a cohesive, undifferentiated social group while the former were the products of a priestly cult in a stratified society where the more basic lineages and families of kin had been replaced by nonkin organized into social groups centered around a town or cult site.

Long before Smith, Ewald and Wellhausen had observed the parallels between Arab Bedouin sacrifice and Hebrew rites.[92] Smith's views were especially influenced by Wellhausen's *Prolegomena:*

There was no such thought as that a definite guilt must and could be taken away by means of a prescribed offering. When the law discriminates between such sins as are covered by an offering and such sins as relentlessly are visited with wrath, it makes a distinction very remote from the antique; to Hebrew antiquity the wrath of God was something quite incalculable, its causes were never known, much less was it possible to enumerate beforehand those sins which kindled it and those which did not. An underlying reference of sacrifice to sin, speaking generally, was entirely absent. The ancient offerings were wholly of a joyous nature — merrymaking before Jehovah with music and song, timbrels, flutes, and stringed instruments. No greater contrast could be conceived than the monotonous seriousness of the so-called Mosaic worship.[93]

In Smith's day his interpretation of sacrifice was a valuable corrective to earlier theories, but his communion theory is seen today to be as inadequate as was Tylor's gift theory. After Smith's death, the great

---

91.   Ibid., pp. 239-40, 244-45, 354-55.

92.   de Vaux, *Studies,* pp. 15-20.

93.   Julius Wellhausen, *Prolegomena to the History of Ancient Israel* (1878; New York: Meridian, 1957), p. 81; compare how similar this is to Smith's characterization ("Sacrifice," p. 134), as well as with his fuller statement (*LRS,* p. 257). Smith's basic views on sacrifice changed little over the years. Black and Chrystal remark that it is strange that his theories on sacrifice were not violently condemned during his trial since they might have been interpreted as heretical (*Life,* pp. 417-18). These had been published widely in *The Old Testament in the Jewish Church* (1881; 2d ed., Edinburgh: A. and C. Black, 1892), pp. 240-53.

Semiticist Salomon Reinach favorably regarded Smith's theory of sacrifice, though an even greater Semiticist, Lagrange, vigorously attacked it in favor of a theory of expiatory oblation.[94] Before World War II, the two standard English surveys of sacrifice in the Old Testament took a synthetic position, trying to combine Smith's communion theory with ones related to the gift, oblation, and expiation theories.[95] Since then critical opinion of biblical scholars has turned even further against Smith. In his useful survey Thompson notes: "Most of the scholars reviewed have conceded that expiation had a larger place in early Israelite sacrifice than the Wellhausen school allowed, but none of them have [sic] devoted to it, a systematic and methodological investigation."[96] Indeed, he provides an extensive list of recent biblical researchers who have found the joyous sacrifice theory untenable and the theme of solemnity and expiation the dominant one in Old Testament sacrifice.[97]

The complex details of these criticisms need not be discussed here. It suffices to note that Smith's use of source material, even in terms of biblical texts, has been shown to be biased. Holocaust, communion, and tribute cannot be neatly separated chronologically as he had supposed, for all aspects seem present at all phases reported. For the most part, Smith's explanations of his negative cases, such as why holocaust was not eaten, simply will not do.[98] On the other hand, when it was later reported that some Australian people did ritually eat their totem, Smith's theory was seen by some as vindicated, even though such practices remain unusual among primitive peoples, even those practicing what was termed *totemism*.

But while his sharp contrast between early communion and later tribute is unacceptable, some of his explanations for these differences reveal a subtle, sociological mind, even while other arguments are inconsistent with this own commitment to explanation in terms of what

94.   Salomon Reinach, "The Growth of Mythological Study," *The Quarterly Review* 429 (October 1911): 423–41; indeed, Reinach called Smith's work brilliant and illuminating, review, p. 158; Lagrange, Etudes, chap. 5, pp. 244-68.

95.   G. B. Gray, *Sacrifice;* Oesterley, *Sacrifices.*

96.   *Penitance and Sacrifice,* pp. 18-19; see also ibid., pp. 21-62, for a survey of the various theories of the origin of Hebrew sacrifice.

97.   Ibid., p. 117.

98.   *LRS,* pp. 388-90.

is meaningful to members of a particular society. An example of the latter is his contention that the concept of expiation was a later rationalization which people attached to communion-type sacrifices when the original and real meaning of these had been forgotten.[99] Durkheim rightly observes: "But it is inadmissible that beliefs and practices as universal as these, which we find at the foundation of the expiatory sacrifice, should be the product of a mere error of interpretation."[100]

An example of Smith's more perceptive insights is his reasoning as to how and why communion sacrifices were replaced in prominence by those associated both with gifts and tribute. He argued that this was due to a new emphasis on the appreciation of material property, implying with this an alienation of the individual from his goods. Thus, this disassociation of property from its owners came about when men no longer sacrificed for and among themselves, but allowed priests and kings to do so for them. By implication this in turn was related to an increased social differentiation and distance, brought on by increased numbers and social density (political amalgamation and a sedentary life) so that gods were alienated from men and became less like kinsmen and more like kings, less among and more apart from men.[101]

A final aspect of Smith's work that is repeatedly taken up (without crediting him) in the French school is his searching consideration of the links between social acts and their physical coordinates. It is precisely in the interplay between the existential but very real forms of social life and the physical world, so real and yet only dimly formed outside social experience, that the most profound symbolic acts occur. Sacrifice epitomizes this in the use of physical properties to assert and maintain moral states. Examples of this may be found in Smith's discussion of food[102] and clothing,[103] and especially in his interpretation of animal sacrifice. He describes concepts as "wrapped in the husk of a material embodiment" and maintains that "a ritual must always remain materi-

99.   Ibid., pp. 347–51.

100.   *Elementary Forms*, p. 412n.

101.   LRS, p. 396; this interpretation has some parallels with de Vaux who associates depersonalization of sacrifice with an increasing dominance of a priesthood (*Studies*, pp. 33–35).

102.   LRS, p. 271; contrast with Durkheim, *Elementary Forms*, p. 235.

103.   LRS, p. 437.

alistic, even if its materialism is disguised under the cloak of mysticism."[104]

Despite the serious flaws in Smith's views of sacrifice, these ideas remain especially important because of the long-term influence they have exerted on three schools of social theory: the French sociologists led by Durkheim, Frazer and his retinue of folklorists and classicists, and the Freudians.

In his preface to *Totemism and Exogamy*,[105] Frazer credits Smith's work on sacrifice with directing his interest toward the study of the slaying of the high god–sacred king. That Smith developed such a notion of sacrifice is not difficult to understand when we remember that he saw his research as illuminating Christianity itself. Christ's own death then constitutes the culmination of the sacrificial notion first appearing in the Old Testament and earlier. In a celebrated passage, removed from the second edition of the *Lectures,* Smith wrote:

The interpretation of the death of the god as corresponding to the annual withering up of nature, which was naturally suggested by the ideas of Baal-worship, effectually shut the door to any ethical interpretation of the annual religious mourning. That the God-man dies for His people, and that His death is their life, is an idea which was in some degree foreshadowed by the oldest mystical sacrifices. It was foreshadowed, indeed, in a very crude and materialistic form, and without any of those ethical ideas which the Christian doctrine of the atonement derives from a profounder sense of sin and divine justice. And yet the voluntary death of the divine victim, which we have seen to be a conception not foreign to ancient sacrificial ritual, contained the germ of the deepest thought in the Christian doctrine: the thought that the Redeemer gives Himself for His people, that "for their sakes He consecrates Himself, that they also might be consecrated in truth." But in Baal-worship, when the death of the god becomes a mere cosmical process, and the most solemn rites that ancient religion knew sank to the level of a scenic representation of the yearly revolutions of the seasons, the features of primaeval ritual which contained germs of better things are effectually hidden out of sight, and the offices of religion cease to

---

104.   Ibid.; Gaster praises Smith's perception in linking communities to their physical and seasonal surroundings; see T. H. Gaster, *Thespis* (1950; paperback ed., New York: Harper, 1966), pp. 22, 46.

105.   *Totemism and Exogamy: A Treatise on Certain Early Forms of Superstition and Society* (1910; rev. ed., London: Macmillan, 1935).

appeal to any higher feeling than that of sympathy with the changing moods of nature.[106]

Here one also senses some uneasiness in that Smith seems to contradict his own theories, for while he wants to consider Christian origins anthropologically, he still must separate his own religious faith from the same type of critical scrutiny that he levels against ancient faiths.

Unfortunately, while Frazer took over this and other themes from Smith, notably those related to the analysis of magic and taboo, he was unable to fit them into any theory of society but rather merely accumulated more and more data within a set of unimaginative and limited descriptive categories.

In contrast, Durkheim was profoundly influenced by Smith, and although critical of some of Smith's views, integrated many into a powerful and persuasive overall view of culture and society.[107] Durkheim is quite explicit regarding Smith's influence. During 1905-7, a Belgian, Simon Deploige, wrote a series of essays maintaining that Durkheim's views on religion and belief derived mainly from Wundt.[108] In a rejoining letter Durkheim remarked:

il est dit que j'aurais trouvé chez Wundt l'idée que la religion est la matrice des idées morales, juridiques etc. C'est en 1887 que je lus Wundt: or c'est seulement en 1895 que j'eus le sentiment net du rôle capital joué par la religion dans la vie sociale. C'est en cette année que, pour la première fois, je trouvai le moyen d'aborder sociologiquement l'étude de la religion. Ce fut pour moi une révélation. Ce cours de 1895 marque une ligne de démarcation dans le développement de ma pensée si bien que toutes mes recherches antérieures durent être reprises à nouveux frais pour être mises en harmonie avec ces vues nouvelles. L'Ethik de Wundt, lue huit ans auparavant, n'était pour rien dans ce changement d'orientation. Il était du tout antieraux études d'historie trauvaux de Robertson Smith et de son école.[109]

106.   LRS, 1st ed., from lecture XI, "Annual Death of the God," p. 393.

107.   These views were also taken up via Durkheim and Frazer, but with no mention of Smith, by F. M. Cornford, *From Religion to Philosophy* (London: E. Arnold, 1912), esp. pp. 73-108.

108.   "La genèse du système de M. Durkheim," *La Revue néo-scolastique* (1905, 1906, 1907).

109.   E. Durkheim, letter, *La Revue néo-scolastique* (1907), p. 613. Durkheim's initial, laconic acknowledgment of his debt to Smith appears in his review of Simon Deploige's *Le Conflit de la morale et de la sociologie* in *L'Année sociologique* 12 (1913): 326-28. In an

Among the aspects of Smith's idea of sacrifice which influenced Durkheim, one of the most questionable was the Wellhausen emphasis on its capacity to produce joyous social integration:

The conception of man's chief good set forth in the social act of sacrificial worship is the happiness of the individual in the happiness of the community, and thus the whole force of ancient religion is directed, so far as the individual is concerned, to maintain the civil virtues of loyalty and devotion to a man's fellows at a pitch of confident enthusiasm, to teach him to set his highest good in the prosperity of the society of which he is a member, not doubting that in so doing he has the divine power on his side and has given his life to a cause that cannot fail. In ancient society, therefore, the religious idea expressed in the act of social worship and the ethical ideal which governed the conduct of daily life were wholly one, and all morality—as morality was then understood—was consecrated and enforced by religious motives and sanctions.[110]

Social ends are reinforced by ritual. Religious behavior is considered not for the beliefs behind it but for the latent functions of ritual, for its conduciveness to fellowship. Durkheim, of course, pursued such analysis throughout his material, whereas Smith modified his perspective once he considered Christianity, though we have seen that he considered common worship as essential as love of God. Unlike Smith, Durkheim's view of the ambiguous and complex relation between the individual and society led him to reject Smith's view that piacular rites were a late development.[111] Durkheim found Smith's views valuable but one-sided.[112] He accepted the communion theory, but only as one aspect of sacrifice. This related to his theory of periodicity, to the revivification of "natural good understanding" through congregation and common physical ritual acts. But for Durkheim oblation and expiation were as important to sacrifice as communion. This oblation allowed the personification of religious forces and was related to the subordination

---

excellent study, Steven Lukes demonstrates Smith's profound influence upon Durkheim (*Emile Durkheim: His Life and Work* [London: Allen Lane the Penguin Press, 1973], pp. 27, 238-39, 241, 244, 450-51, 471). In contrast, no such consideration is given in Dominick LaCapra's disappointing *Emile Durkheim: Sociologist and Philosopher* (Ithaca: Cornell University Press, 1973).

110. *LRS,* p. 267.

111. *Elementary Forms,* p. 406.

112. Ibid., p. 90.

of man to society.[113] If, in communion, persons were enhanced through social fellowship, then through piacular rites individuals were purified socially through altruistic expiation.

For Durkheim, the concept of periodicity was crucial to a solution of Smith's analytical problems, problems which according to Durkheim led to an "inadmissible logical scandal,"[114] namely, Why should gods need men? Durkheim's answer was that gods are manifested through things which in themselves are subject to flux. Men then make offerings because of the instability of the external world, both physical and social (for society too manifests itself physically through persons and things). The gods then are as unstable as men. The stability of either realm is reasserted through symbolic acts, and because this is an illusion, an existential act not really inherent to the nature of things, it must be repeated again and again. Thus Durkheim's uses of Smith's ideas about periodicity, primacy of ritual, and the importance of the "material husk" of symbolic acts all relate to his conception of society itself. Religious rites become the repeated efforts by social men to reassert an illusion by endowing it with the palpability of a physical and group experience. Ironically, Smith's analyses of religious behavior eventually led him back to a consideration of individual consciousness, both in the prophets and ultimately in the development of a Christian conscience; for Durkheim this also led back to the individual, back implicitly to a psychological need for coherence and stability.[115]

Durkheim's evaluation of Smith's work in turn relied upon Hubert and Mauss's reanalysis of sacrifice, and that work, not surprisingly, emphasizes the complexity and ambiguity of the rite. Their view of ritual differs little from Durkheim's, but it would be difficult to determine to what extent each determined the other's position.[116]

Freud's use of Smith's ideas was simpler and yet a greater distortion of Smith's views than was Durkheim's. Freud praised Smith's historical reconstruction of the origin of sacrifice in clan totemism but gave no indication that he was aware that there had been any serious criticisms of this position.[117] He turned Smith's argument about, and what for

---

113. Ibid., p. 344.

114. Ibid.

115. Ibid., p. 347.

116. Ibid., p. 337; Hubert and Mauss, *Sacrifice,* esp. Conclusion.

117. "Totem und Tabu," *Imago,* vol. 2 (1913) — trans., "Totem and Taboo," in *The*

Smith was a cathartic feast cementing society by reaffirming affectual bonds became a guilt-ridden and covertly hostile rite of expiation by which aggression against authority is both denied through taboo and yet reconfirmed through periodic symbolic ingestion of the father in the form of the prohibited taboo object. If Freud's interpretation of sacrifice shares anything with Smith and Durkheim, it is only in centering this act in the psychological tensions produced by the integration of the individual into society and the unresolved perpetuity of these tensions which lead to the periodicity of religious behavior.[118]

Despite Smith's somewhat narrow view of sacrifice, his study unquestionably pointed the way toward a clearer appreciation of that ritual's complexities; for in pursuing his analysis, Smith had tried to determine the relations between pure and impure, sacred and profane. Durkheim notes, "One of the greatest services which Robertson Smith has rendered to the science of religions is to have pointed out the ambiguity of the notion of sacredness."[119] This is clearly illustrated in the difficulties which Smith had in trying to establish distinctions between magic and religion and between taboos toward holiness and those toward pollution.

Religion, Magic, and Taboo

The distinctions which Smith draws between religion and magic stem in large part from the weaknesses in his theory of sacrifice and religion. This, in turn, relates to his commitment to the Wellhausen emphasis upon the positive, group aspects of religion and upon his own essentially optimistic version of Christianity. For Smith, Christianity was the true measure by which all other religions were defined; it was a religion of love, fellowship, joy, and communion with God, with little emphasis upon sin, suffering, and guilt. For him demonic and dangerous powers fell outside the bounds of true religion; these involved superstition. Smith characterized religions as those sets of rituals and beliefs associated with friendly supernatural beings; his concept invoked aspects of love, kinship, community, and sociability. It was "positive" and its roots

Basic Writings of Sigmund Freud, ed. A. A. Brill (New York: Random House, 1938), pp. 811-12.

118. But Freudians did criticize Smith on grounds ironically similar to many theologians, noting that Smith could not deal with guilt and expiation even though these seemed to be prominent features of many sacrifices; see R. E. Money-Kyrle, *The Meaning of Sacrifice* (London: Hogarth, 1930), p. 171.

119. *Elementary Forms*, p. 409.

were in the "orderly and fixed" modes of behavior and thought, which enable man to control himself and his social and physical environment. In contrast, magic related to terror, insecurity, and the individual; it fell outside society. Foreign religious beliefs, desocialized by their diffusion elsewhere in an individualistic and informal manner, also became magical superstitions when held by some within another society originally alien to them. (How Smith could relate this to the heterogeneous roots of Christianity or to its diffusion through missionaries is not clear.) For Smith magic had its roots in the insecurity felt by the individual who had been improperly or inadequately integrated into society; by definition such activities were prompted by alienation, selfishness, and fear.[120] Despite Smith's high appraisal of Hebrew prophets, in general he minimized the individual in Old Testament belief and behavior. This too was clearly the influence of Wellhausen and is today sharply criticized by biblical scholars.[121]

Unfortunately, many anthropologists have tended to persist in making a clearcut distinction between magic and religion, even though both concepts are rooted in profounder elements of cosmology and values. Certainly Durkheim's own distinctions along this line encouraged such an approach. Smith's biases have influenced several generations of anthropological researchers, even though his contrasts between group and individual, positive and negative beliefs have proved to be unproductive and confusing.

Yet even when wrong-headed about his conclusions, Smith always keenly discerned which were the crucial issues to consider. Nowhere are both his perception and his biases more sharply exhibited than in his writing about taboo, which he recognized as evidence of a problem of ambiguity in all socially defined boundaries.[122] He saw that the concepts

120.   *LRS*, pp. 54-55, 89-90, 264-65; Durkheim cites the last passage to support his own categorizations (*Elementary Forms*, p. 45); see also Smith, "Priest," *EB* 19 (1885): 725. For a useful summary of views on the distinctions between magic and religion as these were held in Britain after Smith's death but before Durkheim's main work, see E. S. Hartland, *Ritual and Belief* (London: Williams and Norgate, 1914), esp. "The Relations of Religion and Magic," pp. 26-160. Hartland rejects the interpretation of magic as necessarily individualistic and antisocial. Marett also held to this view, concentrating his criticisms on Frazer but citing Smith most favorably (*Threshold of Religion*, pp. xi, 60).

121.   Thompson, *Penitance and Sacrifice*, pp. 9, 161-62.

122.   Radcliffe-Brown is wrong to credit Frazer rather than Smith with being the first to write systematically about taboo, *Structure and Function*, p. 133.

of holiness and pollution both depended upon restrictive rules of avoidance, and that formally these prohibitions were alike. Without such rules to maintain the integrity of all such categories, they would commingle; through contagion, social and moral qualities would become blurred and thereby jeopardized. This blurring tendency was due to the fact that the categories were social (artificial), and for Smith and Durkheim, a notion like contagion was simply a device for glossing over the implication that these social categories are inevitably subject to erosions and assaults by "natural" reality. Of course, Smith put matters somewhat differently; in words similar to those used by Durkheim in writing about man's subjection to the altruistic conditionings of society, Smith wrote that "holiness is essentially a restriction on the license of man in the free use of natural things."[123] For Smith the ambiguity seems eternal, for "even in some advanced nations the notions of holiness and uncleanness often touch."[124] Despite these observations, Smith seems loathe to credit filth and danger with a truth equal to sacredness. Smith sweeps individuality, guilt, fear, and the appetites beneath a social rug. These were described as lesser aspects of man, and the truer manifestations of religion were presented as the most sociable, least individualistic, and least orectic sides of men. Fear of evil, fear of devils, fear of filth, revulsion and concern over bodily boundaries—all these, for Smith, were manifestations of a consciousness produced at a lower evolutionary level of society. Taboos separating God from man and the profane were positive taboos manifested by a morally and materially advanced society; taboos separating man from misfortune and the embarrassments of his own carnal identity, these were negative taboos signifying a less advanced, fear-ridden social system or, at the least, one insufficiently purified of survivals from an earlier period of lower thought. At such times Smith seems no better in his evaluations than the less informed of his contemporaries who described as "superstitions" those beliefs alien to their own sympathies.[125]

Smith found it difficult to credit what he found morally distasteful as being sacred; he then took the step of equating whatever was sacred

---

123. *LRS,* p. 150.
124. Ibid., p. 153.
125. For Smith's most characteristic statements on taboo, holiness, and pollution, see *LRS,* pp. 152–54, 446–47; Durkheim comments extensively on some of these passages (*Elementary Forms,* pp. 320, 410).

with what was social. What then remained had to be not only polluting and profane but also less social. Durkheim, reading Smith, came to a somewhat similar, though irreligious, conclusion; for him what was truly social must therefore be sacred.

Ritual and Myth

In his brief but excellent survey of the problems associated with the study of ritual, Leach indicates that one of Smith's greatest contributions of his insistence that ritual preceded myth; for Smith symbolic behavior, as acted out, was more meaningful and unvarying through time and place than were the myths and legends sometimes mustered to explain them.[126] Smith, with a Victorian preoccupation with evolutionary origins, maintained not only that ritual was more fundamental than myth, but that it quite literally preceded myth in time. In his attempts to demonstrate this, Smith sometimes committed serious abuses in the comparative method, contending that rites often are not what the actors themselves say they are but that they have other meanings which he could discern through his own comparative research.[127] Had he been our contemporary, doubtless he would have spoken of manifest and latent functions. Clearly, ritual, being a form of symbolic expression, cannot exist without symbols, and this is hardly what Smith seems to have meant. Rather, he did not believe that these symbols were organized into any systematic and well-articulated form. Such systematization came only later with mythological invention and speculative thought. What conceptions men did at first hold received their clearest expression, not in words, but in ritual acts.[128] Metaphorical actions preceded abstract thought. In part Smith was attacking those who sought to analyze and explain ritual through recourse to myths and legends alone, thus making ritual merely magical, mimetic replication of myth.[129]

---

126. *LRS*, p. 399; E. R. Leach, "Ritual," in *Encyclopaedia of the Social Sciences* 13 (1968): 520-26.

127. *LRS*, p. 400.

128. Ibid., pp. 25-26.

129. Indeed, at times Smith tries to explain myths as attempts to rationalize rituals which are still practiced but no longer comprehended, for to him ritual is so essential for social stability that it is performed even when only poorly understood (ibid., pp. 216, 410).

Smith's view was firmly anchored in his conviction that the fundamental source of all symbolic behavior was the social group and that its modes of expression gained their validity from their relation to the readily apprehended world of persons and things. This notion was later expanded by Durkheim, who spent much of his career attacking the baneful influences of the mentalistic utilitarians, such as Bentham; Durkheim clearly derives his concept of symbols from Smith.[130] Although· Smith did not spell this relation out, it rested on a set of assumptions about man's need to conform to certain psychological demands determined by affect and the nature of the senses. Yet these demands were always powerfully channeled by society, sometimes even in the face of "natural" inclinations; for example, "we have already found reason to be chary in assuming that certain acts are natural expressions of sorrow."[131] Perhaps all this remained vague because at other times Smith exhibited some antipathy toward certain individualistic aspects of appetite and affect. Whatever the subtler bases for these complex views, Smith advocated the primacy of ritual, and this had a deeply important impact on the field of cultural anthropology. One effect was to direct the attention of researchers and analysts to the relative social aspects of behavior and to minimize the more absolute, "rational" aspects. Even when and if ideas were examined, this would be insofar as they reflected the shared beliefs of a group. One could no longer simply introspect in Tylorian fashion about the beliefs and behavior of alien peoples. A set of rites was examined in terms of the results which this would have for the group, for its expression of social values and interrelationships. How the particular observer felt about the rationality or reprehensibility of certain practices should, at least theoretically, be of little consequence in estimating their importance in understanding a particular society. The "real" purpose and significance of ritual were different at times even from what the actors themselves believed. It should be clear that such a set of assumptions more readily allowed the relativistic yet comparative approach of a social anthropologist than would assumptions leading first to an analysis of myth and belief, though of course these too are important.

As already noted, Smith was somewhat ill-disposed toward theologians and their emphasis upon a neat theology, at least if this

130.   Ibid, pp. 24-25, 84, 90-91, 213.
131.   *LRS*, p. 433.

distracted believers from fellowship and communal activities. Smith advocated a mastery of the ideas of the church, but he saw theology only as a means, ever developing and being perfected through research and scholarship, for achieving proper Christian social action. Early in his career he expressed a religious view consistent with his sociology: "the Church is not the fellowship of Christian love — which requires no unity of organisation — but the fellowship of Christian worship. The common worship of many individuals must be the expression in intelligible form of their common relation of faith toward God."[132]

The best of Smith's successors have grasped the heuristic advantages of Smith's emphasis upon ritual over myth and belief. For example, Marett, Malinowski, and Radcliffe-Brown praise this side of Smith; Loisy assumes this throughout his work; and it becomes the very heart of most of Durkheim's classic study of religion.[133] In contrast, those inclined toward a psychoanalytical or literary approach remain hostile. Thus, Reik accepts many of Smith's most dubious interpretations of sacrifice and totemism, but questions his de-emphasis of myth. A prominent classicist's recent survey of myth vigorously attacks Smith and others on similar grounds.[134] Of course, in recent years the study of myth has gained a certain vogue, but it can be assumed that before too long this topic will again be placed in more modest perspective within the total picture of religious behavior.

Religion and Society

Smith's single greatest contribution to social research was his emphasis upon the social basis of belief and values. "A man did not choose his religion or frame it for himself; it came to him as part of the general scheme of social obligations and ordinances laid upon him, as a matter of course, by his position in the family and in the nation." "Religion did not exist for the saving of souls but for the preservation and welfare of society."[135] This view was one held from the very beginning of his career

132.   "The Place of Theology in the Work and Growth of the Church," *LE*, p. 329.

133.   Radcliffe-Brown, *Structure and Function*, p. 155; Marett, *Threshold of Religion*, p. 181; Loisy, *Essai*, pp. 1–18.

134.   Reik, *Ritual*, pp. 17–19, 188, 299; G. S. Kirk, *Myth, Its Meaning and Functions in Ancient and Other Cultures* (Cambridge: Cambridge University Press, 1970), pp. 12–13. A similar view is also held by J. E. Fontenrose, *The Ritual Theory of Myth*, Folklore Studies, vol. 18 (Berkeley: University of California Press, 1966).

135.   *LRS*, pp. 28, 29.

when he wrote of "the intimate relation between religion and the fundamental structure of society," crediting McLennan with leading him to such an interpretation.[136] For Smith, society provided the moral qualities that converted mere power into authority; thus supernatural beings recognized within a community who believed in and worshipped them became gods, while those only feared but unworshipped in communal rites were devils; awesome, protective, supernatural power enshrined by society is holiness, while the forces of disorder which society must ward off are pollution; thus communal activities directed toward these beneficent powers embody religion, while individual and less organized activities are mere magic and superstition. For Smith the dichotomy even exists spatially with the protective order of the community contrasted with the disorder of the wilderness.[137]

Smith went on to suggest that man's perception of nature was modeled on his experience in society, that social categories are projected onto the physical, natural world.[138] In this too he clearly influenced Durkheim and expressed a sophistication in the sociology of knowledge far more subtle and insightful than did his contemporaries. His emphasis upon society involves social action, mainly worship, as the key formative process behind belief; this, as we have seen, involved a set of psychological assumptions about the ways group action revivified social bonds by associating evanescent but periodic affectual experiences with more enduring social norms.[139] This interest in the periodicity of affectual reinforcement is in turn loosely related to a theory of the relation between religious activity and social tension and crisis.[140] Religious worship both releases tensions and reinforces weakened social bonds; its effects are both individual and psychological, and also social and communal. The nature of the crisis and the size and complexity of the group involved in turn relate to the character of religious behavior and belief which would be effectual; thus, the larger and more complex

136. *Kinship and Marriage in Early Arabia,* new ed. (Cambridge: Cambridge University Press, 1903), p. 258; see also *The Prophets of Israel,* pp. 96–97.

137. *LRS,* pp. 54–55, 119–22. Evans-Pritchard has sharply criticized Smith's assertion that there is a causal relation between the structure of society and the form of its religious beliefs (*Theories of Primitive Religion,* p. viii).

138. *LRS,* p. 126.

139. *LRS,* pp. 26–30, 263.

140. Ibid., pp. 91–93; Malinowski, *Sex,* p. 254.

a social group, the more sophisticated and, for Smith, morally advanced will be the religion involved.[141] In this crude evolutionism with its simplistic moralistic overtones, Smith is less sophisticated than Fustel de Coulanges writing over twenty years before him.

Despite the distortions and moralistic biases which Smith's models sometimes reflect, they were an enormous improvement over the mentalistic hypothesizing of most of his contemporaries. It can be claimed confidently that Smith is the founder of modern sociology of religion.[142] Smith's work contains many flaws, some due to the prejudices of his time, some due to his own personal involvements in scholarship and religion. Yet no other Victorian seems to have touched upon so many different issues still vital to our anthropological interest, or seems so enduring in the quality and freshness of his insights. Of all the great Victorian anthropologists, he seems nearest to being our contemporary. As Frazer remarked of Smith, "The wonder is not that he did not see further, but that he saw so far.[143]

141. Ibid., pp. 35, 38-40, 47.

142. The only contender to his claim would be Numa Fustel de Coulanges and clearly even in France Fustel's work seems to have had less impact than that of Smith. Despite Steven Luke's contentions to the contrary (*Emile Durkheim,* p. 238), I have not been able to find any influence by Fustel upon Smith or upon McLennan, although obviously Fustel's work is a sociological interpretation that would have pleased Smith.

143. In a letter from Frazer to Stanley Cook, in Cook, "Israel and Totemism," p. 441.

Bibliography

BIOGRAPHICAL MATERIALS

The basic biographical study remains John Sutherland Black and George Chrystal, *The Life of William Robertson Smith* (London: A. and C. Black, 1912). A useful review of this biography and the *Essays* by Stanley A. Cook appears in the *Hibbert Journal* 11 (1912): 211-17. It should be noted that Smith's close friend and biographer, J. S. Black, was no relative of Smith's publishers, even though he was long affiliated with that firm. A short but readily available biography by Emrys Peters, apparently based on the preceding and containing a necessarily cursory evaluation of Smith's work, appears in the *Encyclopaedia of the Social Sciences* (New York: Macmillan, 1968), pp. 329-35. This, however, contains some errors of fact.

The first biography of Smith to be published was a brief essay by John F. White, "William Robertson Smith," *Two Professors of Oriental Languages* (Aberdeen: Aberdeen University Press, 1899), pp. 19-34; a similar short essay by James Bryce is "William Robertson Smith," *Studies in Contemporary Biography* (London: Macmillan, 1903), pp. 311-35. Brief biographical sketches appear in his obituary notices: Edward H. Brown, obituary, *Journal of the Royal Asiatic Society* (1894), pp. 594-603; other obituaries appear in *Cambridge Review* no. 379 (26 April 1894); *The Bookman* no. 32 (May 1894); *Alma Mater* (Aberdeen University) vol. 11, no. 19 (May 1894); and *The Weekly Review* (1894). Norman McLean provides some useful information on Smith's college and university life in *Christ's College Magazine* no. 25 (1894), pp. 99-107. A brief discussion of Smith's achievement in biblical studies is provided in Thomas K. Cheyne, *Founders of Old Testament Criticism* (London: Methuen, 1927), pp. 212-25. Sir James Frazer provides a superficial sketch of his former teacher and mentor in *The Gorgon's Head* (London: Macmillan, 1927), pp. 278-90. A brief biographical sketch entirely dependent on Black and Chrystal's biography appeared to commemorate the centennial of Smith's birth: James B. Pritchard, "W. Robertson Smith, Heretic," *Crozier Quarterly* 24, no. 2 (April 1947): 146–60. Two laudatory biographical sketches by Reverend Charles Earle Raven and Professor Stanley Cook appear in *Aberdeen University Studies* no. 128 (1951). A perceptive biographical sketch emphasizing Smith's Aberdeen trial appears as "Smith o' Aiberdeen," in Donald Carswell, *Brother Scots* (New York: Harcourt, Brace, 1928), pp. 54–120. There is also a very useful set of recollections by one of Smith's fellow students and friends at Aberdeen and Edinburgh, Reverend J. P. Lilley, in "William Robertson Smith: Recollections of a Fellow Student," *The Expositor,* 8th ser., no. 115 (July 1920), pp. 61–75; ibid., no. 116 (August 1920), pp. 126–38. An exceedingly biased and hostile review of Smith by an anonymous "free-thinking" writer with the pen name of Scotulus appears as "Professor Robertson Smith: A Problem," *Free Review* 2 (1 May 1894): 97–107. The most insightful review and appraisal of Smith's work remains Stanley A. Cook, "Introduction," *Lectures on the Religion of the Semites,* 3rd ed.

CHRONOLOGICAL LIST OF WORKS BY SMITH

A full bibliography of Smith's work was published in the *Life*; this includes unpublished papers, lectures, correspondence, and even acknowledgments and dedications by others. Unfortunately, upon checking these sources, I have found this bibliography unreliable and incomplete. I have therefore used the 1912 bibliography only as a working base and have provided corrections, additions, and deletions to bring the bibliography nearer conventional scholarly standards. In large part, Smith's articles in the *Encyclopaedia Britannica* were highly condensed, factual accounts, but some contain the first presentations of his most important theoretical ideas and should be consulted by all interested in exploring his thought. About half of the more than two hundred articles which Smith wrote for the *EB* are unsigned; only those unsigned articles cited by Black and Chrystal may be safely assigned to Smith, and only these are listed in the present bibliography. The offices of the *EB* inform me that there appear to be no surviving records indicating which unsigned articles Smith wrote.

Over the last twelve years of his life Smith envisioned an *Encyclopaedia Biblica* modeled on the *Encyclopaedia Britannica.* Realizing that his health would never allow him to undertake this task, he encouraged his friends T. K. Cheyne and J. S. Black to do so. This monumental work is dedicated to Smith and contains many of Smith's *EB* essays brought up to date by other scholars. See *EBL* 1 (1899): vii–ix.

1868 "Prophecy and Personality." Paper presented at meeting (January) of the New College Theological Society, Edinburgh (unclear whether published). Published as "Prophecy and Personality: a Fragment" in *LE*, pp. 97–108.

"The Work of a Theological Society." Presidential address delivered in November to the New College Theological Society, Edinburgh (unclear whether published). Published in *LE*, pp. 137–62.

1869 "Christianity and the Supernatural." Paper presented at meeting (January) of the New College Theological Society, Edinburgh (unclear whether published). Published in *LE*, pp. 109–36.

"Mr. Mill's Theory of Geometrical Reasoning Mathematically Tested." *Proceedings of the Royal Society of Edinburgh* 6: 477–83. Republished in *LE*, pp. 3–12.

"Hegel and the Metaphysics of the Fluxional Calculus." *Transactions of the Royal Society of Edinburgh* 25, pt. 2: 491–511. Republished in *LE*, pp. 13–43.

"Newton and Hegel." Letter in *Edinburgh Courant,* December 29. (Not obtained.)

1870 "Newton and Hegel." Letter in *Edinburgh Courant,* January 18. (Not obtained.)

"Newton and Hegel." Letter in *Edinburgh Courant,* January 21. (Not obtained.)

"On the Flow of Electricity in Conducting Surfaces." Communicated by Professor Tait February 21. Published in *Proceedings of the Royal Society of Edinburgh* 7 (1872): 79–99. Republished in *LE*, pp. 44–66.

"Prophecy in the Critical Schools of the Continent" (unsigned). *British Quarterly Review* 51, no. 102 (April): 313–43. Republished as "On the Question of Prophecy in the Critical Schools of the Continent" in *LE*, pp. 163–203.

"Note on Professor Bain's Theory of Euclid I.4." Communicated by Professor Tait June 6. Published in *Proceedings of the Royal Society of Edinburgh* 7 (1872): 176-79. Republished in *LE*, pp. 67-75.

What History Teaches Us to Seek in the Bible: A Lecture Delivered at the Opening of the Free Church College, Aberdeen, November 7, 1870. Edinburgh: Edmonston and Douglas. 30 pp. Republished in *LE*, pp. 207-34.

"Extracts from Early Lectures" (1870-1872). In *LE*, pp. 235-52.

1871   "The Fulfilment of Prophecy." In *LE*, pp. 253-84.

Review of *On the Atonement* by Crawford. *Daily Review* (Edinburgh), May 18. (Not obtained.)

"Dutch Periodicals," a review of *Theologisch Tijdschrift* 1871, pts. 1, 2, 3. *BFE* 20 (July): 596-99.

"Old Testament Exegesis," reviews of *The Hebrew Prophets, Translated Afresh from the Original, with Illustrations for English Readers*, vol. 2, by Roland Williams; and *The Minor Prophets, with a Commentary, Explanatory and Practical, and Introductions*, pt. 4, by Rev. E. B. Pusey. *BFE* 20 (July): 596-99.

"On Democratus and Lucretius: A Question of Priority in the Kinetical Theory of Matter" (with T. M. Lindsay). Communications read in Section of Mathematics and Physics of the British Association of Edinburgh. (Not obtained.)

"The Place of the Old Testament in Religious Instruction." In *Proceedings of Fourth Scottish Sabbath School Convention, Which Met at Aberdeen on Wednesday and Thursday, 6th and 7th September, 1871.* Privately printed. Republished as extract in *Prof. W. Robertson Smith on Old Testament Scripture and Theology, Reprint of Newspaper Report of Presentations Made to Professor W. R. Smith by His Students in the Free Church College, Aberdeen (From "Daily Free Press," March 13, 1877)*, pp. 14-23; privately printed. Republished in *LE*, pp. 285-93.

1872   "Dutch Periodicals," a review of *Theologisch Tijdschrift* 1871, pts. 4, 5, 6. *BFE* 21 (January): 162-66.

"Old Testament Exegesis," a review of *Commentaries in Vatacinium Michae* by T. Roorda. *BFE* 21 (April): 388-91.

"On the Value of Critical Study of the Psalms for Their Practical Exposition, Lectures Given at the Free Church College, Aberdeen (January-March)." Published in *LE,* pp. 294-305.

"Church History," a review of *Geschiedkundige Nasporingen* by Christian Sepp. *BFE* 21 (July): 607-12.

1873 "German Periodicals," reviews of *Theologische Studien und Kritiken* 1872, pt. 4; *Jahrbücher für Deutsche Theologie* 1872, pts. 1, 2; *Zeitschrift für Wissenschaftliche Theologie* 1872, pt. 4. *BFE* 22 (January): 171-75.

"Dutch Periodicals," a review of *Theologisch Tijdschrift* 1872, nos. 3-6. *BFE* 22 (January): 175-79.

"Dr. Stirling, Hegel, and the Mathematicians." *Fortnightly Review* 76 (April 1): 495-510. Republished in *LE,* pp. 71-93.

"German and Dutch Periodicals," reviews of *Theologische Studien und Kritiken* 1873, pts. 1, 2; *Jahrbücher für Deutsche Theologie* 1872, pt. 4; *Theologisch Tijdschrift* 1873, pts. 1, 2. *BFE* 22 (April): 376-84.

"German and Dutch Periodicals," reviews of *Studien und Kritiken* 1873, pt. 3; *Jahrbücher für Deutsche Theologie* 1873, no. 1; *Zeitschrift für Wissenschaftliche Theologie* 1873, pt. 2; *Theologisch Tijdschrift* 1873, pt. 3. *BFE* 22 (July): 585-89.

Review of *Die Lehre der Bibel von Gott, oder Theologie des A. und N. B.,* vols. 1, 2, by H. Ewald. *Academy* 4 (October 1): 369-70.

1874 "Dutch and German Periodicals," reviews of *Theologisch Tijdschrift* 1873, pts. 5, 6; *Zeitschrift für Wissenschaftliche Theologie* 1873; *Studien und Kritiken* 1873, pt. 4; *Jahrbücher für Deutsche Theologie* 1873, pts. 2, 3. *BFE* 23 (January): 176-82.

"German Periodicals," a review of *Studien und Kritiken* 1874, pts. 1, 2. *BFE* 23 (April): 375-78.

Review of *An Introductory Hebrew Grammar, with Progressive*

Exercises in Reading and Writing by A. B. Davidson. *BFE* 23 (April): 382-83.

Review of *Modern Doubt* by Christlieb. *Daily Review,* May 15. (Not obtained.)

"The Place of Theology in the Work and Growth of the Church." *BFE* 23 (July): 413-40. Republished in *LE,* pp. 309-40.

"German and Dutch Periodicals" (unsigned), reviews of *Jahrbücher für Deutsch Theologie* 1874, pt. 2; *Theologische Studien und Kritiken* 1874, pt. 4; *Zeitschrift für Wissenschaftliche Theologie* 1874, pt. 3; *Theologisch Tijdschrift* 1874, pts. 4, 5. *BFE* 23 (October): 789-93.

"St. Augustine and His English Translators." *Daily Review,* November. (Not obtained.)

1875 "Old Testament Exegesis" (unsigned), reviews of *De Spreuken van Jezus, den Zoon van Sirach* and *De Apocriefe Boeken des Ouden Verbonds* by Johns. Dyserinck. *BFE* 24 (January): 182-83.

"German Periodicals" (unsigned), reviews of *Zeitschrift für Wissenschaftliche Theologie* 1874, pt. 4; *Jahrbücher für Deutsche Theologie* 1874, pt. 3. *BFE* 24 (January): 157-60.

"German Periodicals" (with J. R.), a review of *Zeitschrift für Wissenschaftliche Jahrbücher für Protestantische Theologie,* no. 1. *BFE* 24 (April): 383-89.

"Dutch Periodicals," a review of *Theologisch Tijdschrift* 1875, pt. 1. *BFE* 24 (April): 389-90.

Review of *Graecus Venetus. Pentateuchi Proverbiorum Ruth Cantici Ecclesiastae Threnorum Danielis Versio Graeca,* ed. Oscar Gebhardt. *BFE* 24 (April): 395-97.

"German Periodicals," a review of "On the Joannine Question" by W. Beyschlag. *BFE* 24 (October): 764-75.

Review of *The Religion of Israel to the Fall of the Jewish State* by A. Kuenen (unsigned). *BFE* 24 (October): 781-85.

Review of *Die Lehre der Bibel von Gott, oder Theologie des A. und N. B.,* vol. 3, by H. Ewald. *Academy* 7 (February 13): 169-70.

"The Origins of the Jewish Week." Letter in *Nature* 11 (March 21): 363.

"Angel." In *EB* 2: 26–28.

"Apostle." In *EB* 2: 194.

"Aramaic Languages." In *EB* 2: 307–8.

"Ark of the Covenant." In *EB* 2: 539.

"Assidaeans" (unsigned). In *EB* 2: 729. Revised posthumous version by T. K. Cheyne, in *EBL,* vol. 1 (1899), column 347.

"Baal." In *EB* 3: 175–76. Revised posthumous version by George F. Moore, in *EBL,* vol. 1 (1899), columns 401–3.

"Bible." In *EB* 3: 634–48.

1876 "On the Name Jehovah (Jahve) and the Doctrine of Exodus III. 14." *BFE* 25 (January): 153–65.

Review of *Servant of Jehovah* by Urwick. *Daily Review,* January 24. (Not obtained.)

Letter in *Daily Review,* June 13. Republished in *Report of College Committee* (Edinburgh: New College). (Not obtained.)

"The Progress of Old Testament Studies." *BFE* 25 (July): 471–93.

Review of *The Principles of Hebrew Grammar* by J. P. N. Land. *Academy* 10 (September 23): 318.

"Canticles." In *EB* 5: 32–36.

"Chronicles, Books of." In *EB* 5: 706–9. Revised posthumous version by Samuel Rolles Driver, in *EBL,* vol. 1 (1899), columns 763–72.

"On Prophecy." Lecture. Published in *LE,* pp. 341–66.

1877 "Altar *Ed.*" Letter in *Daily Review,* March 7. (Not obtained.)

Review of *The Holy Bible, with Various Renderings and Readings from the Best Authorities* by Rev. T. K. Cheyne, S. R. Driver, Rev. R. L. Clarke, and Alfred Goodwin. *Academy* 11 (April 7): 298–300.

Review of *Prophets* by A. Kuenen. *Aberdeen Daily Free Press,* April 20. (Not obtained.)

"The Study of the Old Testament in 1876." *BFE* 26 (October):

779-805. Republished in *LE*, pp. 367-99.

"The Poetry of the Old Testament." *British Quarterly Review* 65 (January): 12-33. Republished in *LE*, pp. 400-451.

Sermon Preached in St. George's Free Church, Edinburgh, on the Afternoon of Sabbath, 27th May 1877. Luke xix. 5. Edinburgh: E. Maclaren and Macniven. 24 pp.

"David." In *EB* 6: 836-42.

"Decalogue." In *EB* 7: 15-17.

"The Colour-Sense of the Greeks." Letter in *Nature* 17 (December 6): 100.

Review of *Levitical Priests* by S. I. Curtiss. *Scotsman*, December 29. (Not obtained.)

"Remarks by Professor W. R. Smith on a Memorandum of the Sub-Committee on the Article 'Bible' in the *Encyclopaedia Britannica*." In *Free Church of Scotland Special Report of the College Committee on Professor Smith's Article "Bible,"* Appendix 2, pp. 19-24. Edinburgh: E. Maclaren and Macniven.

1878 *Answer to the Form of Libel Now before the Free Church Presbytery of Aberdeen (12 February)*. Edinburgh: D. Douglas. 64 pp.

Additional Answer to the Libel, with Some Account of the Evidence That Parts of the Pentateuchal Law Are Later than the Time of Moses (16 April). Edinburgh: D. Douglas. 88 pp.

"Eli." In *EB* 7: 133. Revised posthumous version by T. K. Cheyne, in *EBL*, vol. 2 (1901), columns 1265-66.

1879 Letters from Egypt and Palestine. *Aberdeen Daily Free Press*, January-May. (Not obtained.)

Review of *Geschichte Israels*, vol. 1, by J. Wellhausen. *Academy* 15 (May 17): 429-31. Republished in *LE*, pp. 601-7.

Answer to the Amended Libel; with an Appendix Containing Plea in Law (1 July). Edinburgh: D. Douglas. 42 pp.

1880 "A Journey in the Hejâz." Letters in *Scotsman*, February-June. Republished in *LE*, pp. 487-597.

An Open Letter to Principal Rainy (May 21). Edinburgh:

D. Douglas. 17 pp.

"Animal Tribes in the Old Testament." *Journal of Philology* 19: 75-100. Republished in *LE*, pp. 455-83.

Letter of Professor W. Robertson Smith to Rev. Sir Henry Moncreiff (Aberdeen 21st October 1880). Privately printed. No place. No date. 11 pp.

"Professor de Lagarde's Latest Publications," reviews of *Praetermissorum Libri duo*; *Semitica* 2; *Orientalia liber nunc primum integer et ipso Syriacus*; and *Symmicta* 2 by Paul de Lagarde. *Academy* 18 (November 20): 369-80.

Speech Delivered to a Special Meeting of the Commission of Assembly of the Free Church, on 27th October 1880. Edinburgh: Macniven and Wallace. 32 pp.

"Haggai." In *EB* 11: 370-71. Revised posthumous version by T. K. Cheyne, in *EBL*, vol. 2 (1901), columns 1935-37.

"Hebrew Language and Literature." In *EB* 11: 594-602. Revised posthumous version by A. B. Bruce, in *EBL*, vol. 2 (1901), columns 1984-90.

"Hebrews, Epistle to the." In *EB* 11: 602-7.

"Letter from William Robertson Smith to Dr. Spence, Clerk of Aberdeen Free Presbytery, Dated 17 July 1880." *Scotsman*, July 20.

"Letter from William Robertson Smith to Dr. Binnie, Dated 17 September 1880." "Rejoinder from William Robertson Smith to Dr. Binnie, Dated 22 September 1880." *Scotsman*, September 23.

1881 *The Old Testament in the Jewish Church: Twelve Lectures on Biblical Criticism.* Edinburgh: A. and C. Black (not obtained). American ed. (New York: D. Appleton), xii + 446 pp. 2d ed., rev. and enlarged (London: A. and C. Black, 1892), xiv + 458 pp. Shortened version (New York: G. Munro, 1881), 72 pp. German ed., trans. and Pref. by Prof. Rothstein (1894) (not obtained).

Review of *Gleanings from the Desert of Arabia* by R. D. Upton. *Nature* 24 (July 7): 209-10.

"The Sixteenth Psalm." *Expositor,* 1st ser., 4: 341-72.

"Christ and the Angels (Heb. i)." *Expositor,* 2d ser., 1: 25-33.

"Christ and the Angels (Heb. ii. 1-9)." *Expositor,* 2d ser., 2: 138-47.

"Christ and the Angels (Heb. ii. 10)." *Expositor,* 2d ser., 2: 418-27.

"Hosea." In *EB* 12: 295-98. Revised posthumous version by Karl Marti, in *EBL,* vol. 2 (1901), columns 2119-26.

"Japheth" (unsigned). In *EB* 13: 593.

"Jauhary" (unsigned). In *EB* 13: 598.

"Jerusalem. Section II. Ancient Jerusalem." In *EB* 13: 638-42. Revised posthumous version by George Adam Smith and Claude Reignier Conder, in *EBL,* vol. 2 (1901), columns 2407-32.

"Jiddah" (unsigned). In *EB* 13: 691-92.

"Joel." In *EB* 13: 704-6. Revised posthumous version by Samuel Rolles Driver, in *EBL,* vol. 2 (1901), columns 2492-97.

"Jonah, Rabbi, of Cordova" (unsigned). In *EB* 13: 737-38.

"Jubilee, or Jubile, The Year of" (unsigned). In *EB* 13: 757-58. Revised posthumous version by Immanuel Benzinger, in *EBL,* vol. 2 (1901), columns 2614-16.

"Judges, The Book of." In *EB* 13: 763-64.

1882 *The Prophets of Israel and Their Place in History to the Close of the Eighth Century B. C.* Edinburgh: A. and C. Black. New ed., with Intro. and added notes by T. K. Cheyne (London: A. and C. Black, 1919), lvii + 446 pp.

"The Chronology of the Book of Kings." *Journal of Philology* 10: 61-66.

"Christ and the Angels (Heb. ii. 11-17)." *Expositor,* 2d ser., 3; 63-79.

"Christ and the Angels (Heb. ii. 17, 18)." *Expositor,* 2d ser., 3: 128-39.

"Kings, The First and Second Books of." In *EB* 14: 83-86. Revised posthumous version by E. Kautzsch, in *EBL,* vol. 2 (1901), columns 2664-72.

"Lamentations." In *EB* 14: 240-43. Revised posthumous version by T. K. Cheyne, in *EBL,* vol. 3 (1903), columns 2696-2706.

"Lane, Edward William" (unsigned). In *EB* 14: 282.

"Levites." In *EB* 14: 487-89. Revised posthumous version by Alfred Bertholet, in *EBL,* vol. 3 (1903), columns 2770-76.

"Lokmán" (unsigned). In *EB* 14: 810.

1883 Review of *The Life and Achievement of Edward Henry Palmer* by Walter Besant. *Nature* 28 (July 26): 292-93.

"Notes on Exodus lx. 31, 32." *Journal of Philology* 24: 299-300.

"Lucian, the Martyr" (unsigned). In *EB* 15: 46.

"Mahdí" (unsigned). In *EB* 15: 285.

"Makallá" (unsigned). In *EB* 15: 311.

"Makkarí" (unsigned). In *EB* 15: 311.

"Makrízí" (unsigned). In *EB* 15: 311-12.

"Malachi." In *EB* 15: 313-14. Revised posthumous version by C. C. Torrey, in *EBL,* vol. 3 (1903), columns 2907-10.

"Mas'úddy" (unsigned). In *EB* 15: 623-24.

"Mecca." In *EB* 15: 669-75.

"Medina." In *EB* 15: 817-19.

"Melchizedec" (unsigned). In *EB* 15: 839.

"Mennonites" (unsigned). In *EB* 16: 11-12.

"Meroe" (unsigned). In *EB* 16: 40-41.

"Messiah." In *EB* 16: 53-56. Revised posthumous version by E. Kautzsch and T. K. Cheyne, in *EBL,* vol. 3 (1903), columns 3057-64.

"Micah." In *EB* 16: 224-26. Revised posthumous version by T. K. Cheyne, in *EBL,* vol. 3 (1903), columns 3068-74.

"Michaelis, Johann David" (unsigned). In *EB* 16: 227-28.

"Michmash" (unsigned). In *EB* 16: 241. Revised posthumous version by T. K. Cheyne, in *EBL,* vol. 3 (1903), columns 3078-79.

"Midian" (unsigned). In *EB* 16: 284.

"Mochá" (unsigned). In *EB* 16: 540.

"Moloch." In *EB* 16: 695–96.

"The Theological Chairs." Letter in *Scotsman,* March 30. (Not obtained.)

1884 "The Attitude of Christians to the Old Testament." *Expositor,* 2d ser., 7: 241–51.

"Mohammedan Mahdis." *Good Words* 25: 531, 620. (Not obtained.)

"Motonabbi" (unsigned). In *EB* 17: 1.

"Muscat" (unsigned). In *EB* 17: 64–65.

"Nabataeans" (unsigned). In *EB* 17: 160. Revised posthumous version by T. K. Cheyne, in *EBL,* vol. 3 (1903), columns 3254–55.

"Nahum." In *EB* 17: 165.

"Nazarite" (unsigned). In *EB* 17: 303. Revised posthumous version by T. K. Cheyne, in *EBL,* vol. 3 (1903), columns 3362–64.

"Ninevah." In *EB* 17: 511–12.

"Numerals." In *EB* 17: 624–27.

"Obadiah." In *EB* 17: 702–3. Revised posthumous version by T. K. Cheyne, in *EBL,* vol. 3 (1903), columns 3454–62.

1885 *Kinship and Marriage in Early Arabia.* Cambridge: Cambridge University Press. xv + 320 + 20 pp. 2d ed., with added notes by author and Ignácz Goldziher, ed., and with Preface by Stanley A. Cook (London: A. and C. Black, 1903), xxii + 325. Reissued (Oosterhout N. B., Netherlands: Anthropological Publications, 1966). American ed., with Preface by Emrys L. Peters (Boston: Beacon Press, 1967), xxv + 324 pp.

"Old Testament Notes." *Journal of Philology* 25: 61–66.

"On the Forms of Divination and Magic Ennumerated in Deut. xviii. 10, 11." *Journal of Philology* 26: 273–87; 27: 113–28.

Preface to the English trans. of *Prolegomena to the History of Ancient Israel* by Julius Wellhausen, pp. v–x. London: A. and C. Black. Reprinted (New York: Meridian, 1957). 1957).

"Palmer, Edward Henry" (unsigned). In *EB* 18: 192.

"Palmyra." In *EB* 18: 198-203.

"Paradise" (unsigned). In *EB* 18: 236-37.

"Passover and Feast of Unleavened Bread." In *EB* 18: 343-44.

"Pellicanus, Conrad" (unsigned). *EB* 18: 477-78.

"Petra." In *EB* 18: 705-6.

"Philistines." In *EB* 18: 755-57.

"Phoenix." In *EB* 18: 810-11.

"Pico, Giovanni of Mirandola" (unsigned). In *EB* 19: 80-81.

"Pocock, Edward" (unsigned). In *EB* 19: 252-53.

"Polyglott" (unsigned). In *EB* 19: 417.

"Priest." In *EB* 19: 724-30. Revised posthumous version by Alfred Bertholet, in *EBL,* vol. 3 (1903), columns 3901-5.

"Proselyte" (unsigned). In *EB* 19: 823-24. Revised posthumous version by W. H. Bennett, in *EBL,* vol. 3 (1903), columns 3901-5.

1886 "Richteren ix. 28" (Judges lx. 28). *Theologisch Tijdschrift* 20: 195-98.

Review of *Studies in Ancient History,* new ed., by J. F. McLennan. *Nature* 35 (November 4): 3-4.

"Psalms, Book of." In *EB* 20: 29-34. Revised posthumous version by T. K. Cheyne, in *EBL,* vol. 3 (1903), columns 3921-67.

"Reuchlin, John." In *EB* 20: 489-91.

"Ruth, Book of." In *EB* 20: 110-12. Revised posthumous version by T. K. Cheyne, in *EBL,* vol. 4 (1903), columns 4165-72.

"Sabbath." In *EB* 21: 124-27. Revised posthumous version by Karl Marti and T. K. Cheyne, in *EBL,* vol. 4 (1903), columns 4173-80.

"Sacrifice." In *EB* 21: 132-38.

"Salt (Ancient History)." In *EB* 21: 234. Revised posthumous version by A. R. S. Kennedy, in *EBL,* vol. 4 (1903), columns 4247-50.

"Samaria" (unsigned). In *EB* 21: 243-44.

"Samaritans" (unsigned). In *EB* 21: 244-46.

"Samuel, Books of" (unsigned). In *EB* 21: 252-53.

"Semiramis" (unsigned). In *EB* 21: 639-40.

"Shiloh" (unsigned). In *EB* 21: 803.

1887 "Ctesias and the Semiramis Legend." *English Historical Review* 2, no. 6 (April): 303-17.

"Captain Conder and Modern Criticism." *Contemporary Review* 51 (April): 561-69.

"On the Hebrew root קצע and the Word טקצוע ." *Journal of Philology* 16: 71-81.

"Archaeology and the Date of the Pentateuch." *Contemporary Review* 52 (October): 491-503.

"Socotra" (unsigned). In *EB* 22: 231.

"Suakim" (unsigned). In *EB* 22: 615.

"Suez" (unsigned). In *EB* 22: 620-21.

"Sylburg, Friedrich" (unsigned). In *EB* 22: 809.

"Synagogue" (unsigned). In *EB* 22: 811-12.

"Synedrium" (unsigned). In *EB* 22: 812. Revised posthumous version by M. A. Cannery, in *EBL,* vol. 4 (1903), columns 4840-44.

1888 "On the Sacrifice of a Sheep to the Cyprian Aphrodite: Abstract of a Paper Given before the Cambridge Philological Society on 26 January 1888." *Cambridge University Reporter.* Published in full as note G, *Lectures on the Religion of the Semites,* 2d ed.

Review of *Histoire du peuple d'Israël* by E. Rennan, vol. 1. *English Historical Review* 3, no. 9 (January): 127-35. Republished in *LE,* pp. 608-22.

"The Route from Syria to Egypt." Letter in *Academy* 33 (February 25): 133-34.

Review of *Geschichte der Hebräer,* vol. 1, by R. Kittel. *English Historical Review* 3, no. 10 (April): 351-52.

"Tabernacle" (unsigned). In *EB* 23: 5-6.

"Tabernacles, Feast of" (unsigned). In *EB* 23: 6.

"Tarsus" (unsigned). In *EB* 23: 67-68.

"Temple." In *EB* 23: 165-67.

"Tischendorf, Lobegott Friedrich Konstantin" (unsigned). In *EB* 23: 409.

"Tithes." In *EB* 23: 410-11.

"Tobit, The Book of." In *EB* 23: 427-28.

"Valle, Pietro della" (unsigned). In *EB* 24: 43-44.

"Volusenus, Florentius" (unsigned). In *EB* 24: 296.

"Vow." In *EB* 24: 300-301.

"Walton, Brian" (unsigned). In *EB* 24: 341-42.

"Zephaniah." In *EB* 24: 780-81. Revised posthumous version by Samuel Rolles Driver, in *EBL,* vol. 4 (1903), columns 5402-8.

"Preface." In *EB* 25: v-vi.

1889 *Lectures on the Religion of the Semites: First Series, The Fundamental Institutions.* Edinburgh: A. and C. Black. xii + 488 pp. 2d ed., rev., ed. J. S. Black (London: A. and C. Black,1894), xiv + 507 pp. New ed., same as 2d ed., rev. (London: A. and C. Black, 1923). 3d ed., same as 2d ed. with Introduction by Stanley A. Cook (London: A. and C. Black, 1927). American ed. (New York: Appleton, 1889), 488 pp. 2d American ed. (New York: Macmillan, 1927). 3d American ed. with Prolegomena by James Muilenberg (New York: Ktav, 1969). American paperback eds. (New York: Meridian, 1956; New York: Schocken, 1972). German trans. by R. Stübe, with Preface by E. Kautzsch, *Die Religion der Semiten* (Freiburg en Brisgau, 1899) (not obtained).

"Professor Sayce's Critique of *The Religion of the Semites.*" Letter in *Academy* 36 (December 27): 374-75.

1890 Review of *History of Phoenicia* by George Rawlinson. *English Historical Review* 5, no. 17 (January): 125-27.

Preface and annotations (as vol. editor) for *Lectures on the Comparative Grammar of Semitic Languages: From the Papers of the Late William Wright, LL.D.* Cambridge: Cambridge University Press.

"On the Route from Amorion to Melagina as Given by Edrisi, but More Correctly by Ibn-Khordadhbeh." Note in *Historical*

Geography of Asia Minor by Sir W. M. Ramsay, p. 445. Royal Geographical Society Supplementary Papers 4.

1891 Review of *The History of Human Marriage* by Edvard Westermarck. *Nature* 44 (July 23): 270–71.

"On ΘαλατΘ in Berosus." *Zeitschrift der deutschen Morgandländischen Gesellschaft*, September. (Not obtained.)

1892 "Aus einem Briefe von W. Robertson Smith von 27. 8. 91. (mitgeteilt von K. Budde) (Ex. 21, 8; 21, 22)." *Zeitschrift für alttestamentliche Wissenschaft* (Giessen), 12: 162–63.

"Notes on Hebrew Words." *Jewish Quarterly Review* 4: 289–92.

1893 Review of *Geschichte der Hebräer*, vol. 2, by R. Kittel. *English Historical Review* 8, no. 30 (April): 314–16.

"Remarks on Mr. Kay's Edition of Omārah's History of Yemen." *Journal of the Royal Asiatic Society*, April, pp. 181–217.

"Report on Haematite Weight, with an Inscription in Ancient Semitic Characters, Purchased at Samaria in 1890 by Thomas Chaplin, Esq., M.D." *Academy* 44 (November 18): 443–45.

"Appendix on the Nations Surrounding Israel." In *Cambridge Companion to the Bible for Schools and Colleges*, pp. 109–14. Cambridge: Cambridge University Press.

1896– *A Grammar of the Arabic Language*, 2 vols., revised, enlarged,
1898 and translated from the work of Carl Paul Caspari (*Grammatik der Arabischen Sprache*), by William Wright. 3d edition, enlarged and edited by W. R. Smith and Michiel Jande de Goeje. London: Cambridge University Press.

1912 *Lectures and Essays of William Robertson Smith*. Edited by John Sutherland Black and George Chrystal. London: A. and C. Black. xii + 622 pp.

Notes

Smith is purported by Black and Chrystal to have had an extensive influence in amending the texts of two volumes in the *Smaller Cambridge Bible for Schools and Colleges*. Unfortunately, I could find no mention of Smith in either of these volumes: *The Book of Joshua*, ed. Rev. G. P. Maclear, and *The Book of Judges*, ed. J. J. Lias, vols. 39 and 40 of *Smaller Cambridge Bible for Schools and Colleges* (London: Cambridge University Press, 1891, 1893).

Regarding Smith's editorship of the Caspari-Wright grammar of Arabic, 1896–98, William Wright, Smith's predecessor in the Sir Thomas Adams Chair in Arabic at Cambridge, translated, edited, and revised two editions of Carl Paul Caspari's *Grammar,* and in view of its expansion, it virtually became Wright's own work. After Wright's death, Smith was asked to prepare a third edition, but he died when only fifty-six pages were in manuscript form. Smith's friend, Professor de Goeje, became the new editor. According to him, few notes by Smith were available for the unprepared sections, but where these did exist, they were subsequently published with Smith's initials. A fourth edition, edited by A. A. Bevan, was published in 1932; this is said to be very close to the third edition and contains the prefaces to the second and third.

LITERATURE RELATED TO SMITH'S TRIAL

All of the material cited below is available in the National Library of Scotland in Edinburgh. I have divided the source material into three sections: (1) reports of the official and semiofficial reactions within the Free Church; (2) polemical books, pamphlets, and letters published in reaction to Smith; (3) local newspaper accounts of the events related to the trial. In those cases where the author of the material has used a pseudonym or published anonymously but where his identity is known, I provide his name in brackets. I have annotated some of the entries where this seemed useful. I make no claim to completeness for this bibliography.

Reports of the Official and Semioffical Reactions within the Free Church

Anonymous. *Professor W. Robertson Smith: Report of the Speeches Delivered at a Meeting of Free Church Office-Bearers Who Disapproved of the Action of the Commission in the Case of Prof. W. Robertson Smith: Held in the Christian Institute, Glasgow, Friday, December 3rd, 1880.* Glasgow: W. G. Blackie, 1881.

A pamphlet contending that the church commission exceeded its powers and that it was highly biased against Smith.

————. *Professor W. Robertson Smith on Old Testament Scripture and Rationalistic Theology: Reprint of Newspaper Report of Presenta-*

tions Made to Professor W. R. Smith, by His Students in the Free Church College, Aberdeen. Privately printed, n.p., n.d.
A pamphlet containing speeches by Smith's students and also one of Smith's essays. The speeches were previously printed in the *Daily Free Press,* 13 March 1877.

Blackie, W. G. *Professor W. Robertson Smith: The Action of the Free Church Commission Ultra Vires: A Reply to the "Action of the Committee Vindicated" by the Rev. J. Adam.* Glasgow: D. D. Blackie and Son, D. Bryce, 1881.

Free Church of Scotland. *The Libel against Professor William Robertson Smith: Report of Proceedings into the Free Church Presbytery of Aberdeen, Feb. 14, to March 14, 1878, with Form of Libel.* Aberdeen: Murray; Edinburgh: E. Maclaren and Macniven; Glasgow: D. Bryce, 1878.

————. *Special Report of the College Committee on Professor Smith's Article "Bible."* Edinburgh: E. Maclaren and Macniven, 1877.
A useful pamphlet providing a list of the commissioners and containing various dissenting opinions and a defense by Smith.

————. *Reports and Sketches of the General Assembly of 1880* (not obtained).

Polemical Books, Pamphlets, and Letters
Published in Reaction to Smith

Anonymous. *Chronicles and Canticles.* Scottish Tracts for the Times, no. 5. Edinburgh: Macniven and Wallace, 1880.
A pamphlet criticizing Smith's *Encyclopaedia* articles on these topics.

————. *The Fallibility of Inspired Scripture, as Maintained by Modern Criticism: Being an Examination of Views Propounded by Professor W. R. Smith, of Aberdeen, in Their Bearing in the Doctrine of Inspiration.* Glasgow: D. Bryce; Edinburgh: E. Maclaren and Macniven; Aberdeen: A. and R. Milne; London: J. Nisbet, 1877.

————. *The Free Church and the Higher Criticism: Being a Letter to Professor W. R. Smith on Subjects Treated in His Contributions to the New Edition of the "Encyclopaedia Britannica," by a Layman.* Glasgow: D. Bryce; Edinburgh: E. Maclaren and Macniven, 1877.

————. *Higher Criticism Principles and Practices: An Appeal to Members of All Christian Churches, Regarding the Questions Raised by Professor Smith's Article "Bible" and Others in the New Edition of the "Encyclopaedia Britannica" being a Sequel to "The Free Church and the Higher Criticism" by a Layman.* Glasgow: D. Bryce; Edinburgh: E. Maclaren and Macniven; Aberdeen: A. and R. Milne, 1877.

————. *The New Lines and the Old; or, The Evangelical Outlook in Scotland, in Some Letters from a Scot at Home to a Scot Abroad.* London: J. Nisbet; Edinburgh: E. Maclaren, 1881.

A pamphlet discussing the dangers of outside influences and the new biblical criticism; very anti-Smith.

————. *A Purteekler Account o' the Last Assembly by Wan o' the Hielen'host.* Edinburgh: J. Gemmell, 1881.

A crude anti-Smith tract.

————. *Should Professor Smith Be Removed from His Chair? Extracts from the Article "Hebrew Language and Literature" in Volume XI of the "Encyclopaedia Britannica," with Observations on These Extracts.* N.p., n.d.

Anonymous [Bell, A. Taylor]. *Letters from the Red Beech: Six Letters by a Layman to a Minister of the Free Church of Scotland on the Canon, the Pulpit, and Criticism.* Edinburgh: E. Maclaren, 1881.

A pamphlet reflecting public perplexity over the Smith case and general dissatisfaction with the church committee.

———— [Bell, Benjamin]. *Thoughts on the Aberdeen Case by a Pre-Disruption Elder.* Edinburgh: E. Maclaren, 1880.

———— [Darby, John Nelson]. *Have We a Revelation from God? Being a Review of Professor Smith's Article "Bible," in the Encyclopaedia Britannica.* London: Office of the Bible Witness, 1877.

An anti-Smith book compiled from articles appearing in the *Bible Witness and Review* (London).

———— [Montgomery, Rev. John]. *An Examination of Articles Contributed by Professor W. Robertson Smith to the Encyclopaedia Britannica, The Expositor and the British Quarterly Review, in Relation to the Truth, Inspiration, and Authority of the Holy Scriptures. By a Minister of the Free Church of Scotland.* Edinburgh: J. Gemmell, 1877.

———— [Montgomery, Rev. John]. *Professor Smith and His Apologists: A Few Words Concerning a Pamphlet Entitled "The Authority of Scripture Independent of Criticism," by James Candlish, D.D., and a Pamphlet Entitled "A Plain View of the Case of Professor W. Robertson Smith" by the Rev. Wm. Miller, M.A., with an Appendix, Containing Remarks on the Article, "Apocrypha," by Professor A. B. Davidson, in the New Edition of the "Encyclopaedia Britannica," by a Minister of the Free Church of Scotland.* Edinburgh: J. Gemmell, 1878.

———— [Walker, Rev. W.]. *Moses and Deuteronomy; or, The Present State of the Question as to the Date and Authorship of the Book of Deuteronomy by Moderator.* Edinburgh: John Menzies; Aberdeen: Andrew Elliot, 1880.

———— [Watson, James]. *The Present Position of Professor Robertson Smith's Case, with Reference to Letters by Sir Henry W. Moncreiff in the "Weekly Review" by a Free Church Layman.* Edinburgh: Ballantyne, Hanson, 1879.

———— [Watson, John]. *The Robertson Smith Case: Recorded Reasons and Imputed Motives by the Free Church Leaders by a Free Church Layman.* Edinburgh: Ballantyne, Hanson, 1882.

———— [Wilson, Robert]. *The Bible on the Rock: A Letter to Principal Rainy, on His Speech in the Free Church Commission, and on Professor W. R. Smith's Articles in the "Encyclopaedia Britannica," by the Author of "The Sabbath on the Rock."* Edinburgh: J. Gemmell, 1877.

Bannerman, Rev. D. *The Present Position of the Case of Professor Robertson Smith: A Speech Delivered in the Free Presbytery of Perth, March 30, 1881.* Edinburgh: Andrew Elliot, 1881.

Binnie, William. *The Proposed Reconstruction of the Old Testament History.* Edinburgh: Andrew Elliot, 1880.
     An anti-Smith pamphlet by one of Smith's colleagues at the Free Church College, Aberdeen.

Bonar, Rev. Andrew A. *A Protest for Reverence.* Scottish Tracts for the Times, no. 7. Edinburgh: Macniven and Wallace, 1880.

Candlish, James S. *The Authority of Scripture Independent of Criticism.* Edinburgh: A. and C. Black, 1877.
     One of the very few pamphlets which is pro-Smith, published by

the firm that was to become Smith's supporters and publishers.

Donaldson, Rev. John. *The Question Was Moses the Author of the Pentateuch? Answered in the Affirmative by Herman Witsius.* Edinburgh: E. Maclaren and Macniven; Glasgow: D. Bryce; London: A. and R. Milne, n.d.

A pamphlet using an outdated Continental scholar to prove Smith wrong, making use of a chapter from Herman Witsius, *Miscellanea* (Amsterdam, 1691).

Douglas, C. M. *Why I Still Believe That Moses Wrote Deuteronomy: Some Reflections after Reading Professor Robertson Smith's Additional Answer to the Libel.* Edinburgh: E. Maclaren and Macniven, 1878.

An anti-Smith book by a professor of Hebrew at Glasgow.

Forwell, Rev. William. *Remarks on Professor Smith's Theory of Scripture.* Edinburgh: J. Menzies, 1881.

Green, Rev. W. H. *Professor Robertson Smith on the Pentateuch.* London: J. Nisbet, 1882.

An anti-Smith booklet with a prefatory note by Rev. A. H. Charteris, the biblical scholar whose adverse review of one of Smith's essays precipitated the controversy.

Innes, A. Taylor. *The Assembly of 1881 and the Case of Professor Robertson Smith.* Edinburgh: E. Maclaren, 1881.

————. *The Confidence of the Church: A Letter to Sir Henry W. Moncreiff.* Edinburgh: E. Maclaren, 1881.

A pamphlet addressed to one of Smith's major official attackers.

Innes, James. *The Commission of Assembly and Professor R. Smith's Reply to the Committee's Report.* Edinburgh: E. Maclaren, 1881.

Kennedy, James. *Observations on Professor W. R. Smith's Article "Bible" in the Encyclopaedia Britannica.* Edinburgh: J. Gemmell, 1877.

Kidston, Mr. *Speech of Mr. Kidston, Ferniegair, in Regard to Professor Smith's Recent Letter.* N.p., 1880.

Lyell, Andrew (pseudonym for John Skelton). *The Sergeant in the Hielands.* Edinburgh: W. Blackwood, 1881.

A gross, crude satire against Smith which particularly offended him.

Macaulay, Rev. George. *"Hebrew Language and Literature," Professor Robertson Smith's New Ideas Considered.* Edinburgh: G. Adam Young, n.d.

———. *"Hebrew Language and Literature," Professor Robertson Smith's "Scientific Convictions" and Critical Inventions Examined.* Edinburgh: G. Adam Young, n.d.

———. *Professor Smith's Obligations to Dr. Kuenen Indicated by Rev. George Macauley.* Edinburgh: Lyon and Gemmell, 1876.
A pamphlet attacking the illustrious Dutch biblical scholar, Kuenen, as a means of discrediting Smith.

Miller, Rev. William. *A Plain View of the Case of Professor W. Robertson Smith.* Edinburgh: E. Maclaren and Macniven, 1877.

M. N. (pseudonym for James Kennedy). *Remarks on Professor W. R. Smith's Article "Bible" in the Encyclopaedia Britannica, Ninth Edition.* Edinburgh: Lyon and Gemmell, 1876.

Mnason (pseudonym for William P. Smith). *"The Bible," by Rev. Walter Wood: Examined by Mnason.* Scottish Tracts of the Times, no. 1. Aberdeen: Alexander Murray, 1880.
Smith's father defends his son's views by criticizing a pamphlet which had attacked Smith.

Moncreiff, Rev. Sir Henry W. *Communication on the Case of Professor Robertson Smith, in the General Assembly of the Free Church of Scotland, Held at Glasgow in 1878. By Rev. Sir Henry Wellwood Moncreiff and Others, Reprinted from the "London Weekly Review" (July and August 1879), also An Additional Communication by Sir Henry Moncreiff Reprinted from the "Weekly Review" (Jan. 1879).* Edinburgh: E. Maclaren; Glasgow: D. Bryce; Aberdeen: A. and R. Milne, 1879.

———. *History of the Case of Professor W. Robertson Smith in the Free Church of Scotland, from Its First Consideration by the College Committee till the Close of the General Assembly in 1879.* Edinburgh: E. Maclaren, 1879.
Two books by one of the most vehement and reactionary of Smith's detractors.

———. *Justice of Procedure in the Free Assembly: A Reply to Mr. Taylor Innes to Which Is Annexed a Correspondence with Dr. Anderson Kirkwood.* Edinburgh: E. Maclaren, 1881.

A pamphlet in reply to Innes's criticisms that the procedures against Smith were poorly conducted.

Murray, Rev. Thomas. *Nineteenth Century Unbelief: With Addendum Bearing on the Free Church Crisis.* Aberdeen: James Murray; Edinburgh: E. Maclaren; Glasgow: D. Bryce; London: J. Nisbet, 1879.

Paul, Rev. William. *The Authorship and Date of the Books of Moses Considered with Special Reference to Professor Smith's Views.* Aberdeen: Lewis Smith, 1878.

Sime, James. *Uncritical Criticism: A Review of Professor W. Robertson Smith's Committee Speech.* Edinburgh: E. Maclaren, 1881.

Smith, Rev. James. *Professor Smith's New Plea and the Presbytery's Procedure: Being the Substance of a Speech Delivered in the Free Synod of Aberdeen, 14th October 1879.* Edinburgh: J. Gemmell, 1879.

―――. *Professor Smith on the Bible, and Dr. Marcus Dods on Inspiration.* Edinburgh: John Greig, 1877.

Smith, Rev. Stevenson. *A Review of Professor Smith's Article on Hebrew Language and Literature.* Edinburgh: E. Maclaren; Glasgow: D. Bryce, 1880.

Stuart, A. Moody. *The Fifty-First Psalm and the Encyclopaedia Britannica.* Edinburgh: E. Maclaren and Macniven, 1876.

―――. *Our Old Bible: Moses on the Plains of Moab.* Edinburgh: E. Maclaren, 1879.

Symington, Alexander Macleod. *Angels, with Reference to the Article by Professor Smith in the Ninth Edition of the Encyclopaedia Britannica.* Edinburgh: Macniven and Wallace, 1880.

―――. *Eve with Reference to the Article by Professor W. R. Smith in the Encyclopaedia Britannica.* Edinburgh: Macniven and Wallace, 1880.

Thomas, John. *Wellhausen and Our Higher Criticism.* Scottish Tracts for the Times, no. 5. Edinburgh: Macniven and Wallace, 1880.

A pamphlet attacking the famous German biblical scholar and Semiticist and thereby attacking Smith who had based much of his work on such studies.

Walker, Rev. N. L. *What Is Being Said in America.* Scottish Tracts for the Times, no. 6. Edinburgh: Macniven and Wallace, 1880. A pamphlet discussing reactions in America to Smith and the new biblical criticism.

Watts, Robert. *The New Apologetic and Its Claims to Scriptural Authority.* Edinburgh: E. Maclaren, 1879.

————. *The Newer Criticism and the Analogy of the Faith: A Reply to Lectures by W. Robertson Smith, M.A., on the Old Testament in the Jewish Church.* Edinburgh: T. and T. Clark, 1881. Two anti-Smith books by a theologian in Belfast.

White, Rev. Malcolm. *Professor W. R. Smith's Article on "Hebrew Language and Literature" in the Eleventh Volume of the Encyclopaedia Britannica.* Edinburgh: E. Maclaren, 1880.

Whitemore, C. J. *The Bible in the Furnace: A Review of Prof. W. R. Smith's Article "Bible" in the "Encyclopaedia Britannica."* Edinburgh: E. Maclaren and Macniven; Glasgow: D. Bryce; London: J. Nisbet; Aberdeen: A. and R. Milne, 1877.

Local Newspaper Accounts

Daily Review (Edinburgh), 14 July 1880; 28 October 1880; 17, 18, 20 November 1880; 2, 3 December 1880.

Glasgow Herald, 25 May 1881.

The Scotsman (Edinburgh), 27, 28, 29, 30, 31 May 1879; 2 June 1879; 12, 20, 21 August 1880; 20, 23 September 1880; 15, 16, 17, 18, 20, 22, 23, 25 November 1880; 24 May 1881; 10, 17, 23, 24 June 1881.